Company's Coming

School Days Lunches

Jean Paré

www.companyscoming.com
visit our website

Front Cover

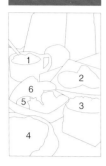

1. Tortellini And Tomato Sauce, page 62
2. Chicken Cheese Pitas, page 34
3. Hit-The-Trail Mix, page 104
4. Spinach Fruit Salad, page 22
5. Apple Cinnamon Dip, page 113
6. Banana Bread Dunkers, page 110

Back Cover

Top: Iced Apple Tea, page 12
Bottom: Sprinkle Cookies, page 112

Sixth Printing August 2006

Library and Archives Canada Cataloguing in Publication
Paré, Jean, date
School days lunches / Jean Paré.
(Original series)
Includes index.
ISBN 13: 978-1-896891-77-4
ISBN 10: 1-896891-77-2
1. Lunchbox cookery. I. Title. II. Series: Paré, Jean.
Original series.
TX735.P38 2005   641.5'34   C2004-907423-7

Published by
Company's Coming Publishing Limited
2311 – 96 Street
Edmonton, Alberta, Canada T6N 1G3
Tel: 780-450-6223   Fax: 780-450-1857
www.companyscoming.com

Company's Coming is a registered trademark owned by Company's Coming Publishing Limited

Printed in Canada

We gratefully acknowledge the following suppliers for their generous support of our Test and Photography Kitchens:

Broil King Barbecues
Corelle®
Hamilton Beach® Canada
Lagostina®
Proctor Silex® Canada
Tupperware®

Our special thanks to the following businesses for providing props for photography:

Canadian Tire
Canhome Global
Casa Bugatti
Danesco Inc.
Island Pottery Inc.
Pfaltzgraff Canada
Scholar's Choice
Wal-Mart Canada Inc.
Zellers

Need more recipes?

Six *"sneak preview"* recipes are featured online **with every new book released.**

Visit us at

www.companyscoming.com

Company's Coming Cookbooks

Original Series

- Softcover, 160 pages
- 6" x 9" (15 cm x 23 cm) format
- Lay-flat plastic comb binding
- Full-colour photos
- Nutrition information

Quick & easy recipes! Everyday ingredients!

Lifestyle Series

- Softcover, 160 pages
- 8" x 10" (20 cm x 25 cm) format
- Paperback
- Full-colour photos
- Nutrition information

Most Loved Recipe Collection

- Hardcover, 128 pages
- 8 3/4" x 8 3/4" (22 cm x 22 cm) format
- Durable sewn binding
- Full-colour throughout
- Nutrition information

Special Occasion Series

- Hardcover & softcover
- 8 1/2" x 11" (22 cm x 28 cm) format
- Durable sewn binding
- Full-colour throughout
- Nutrition information

See page 125 for more cookbooks.
For a complete listing, visit
www.companyscoming.com

Table of Contents

The Company's Coming Story

Jean Paré (pronounced "jeen PAIR-ee") grew up understanding that the combination of family, friends and home cooking is the best recipe for a good life. From her mother, she learned to appreciate good cooking, while her father praised even her earliest attempts in the kitchen. When Jean left home, she took with her a love of cooking, many family recipes and an intriguing desire to read cookbooks as if they were novels!

> **"never share a recipe you wouldn't use yourself"**

In 1963, when her four children had all reached school age, Jean volunteered to cater the 50th Anniversary of the Vermilion School of Agriculture, now Lakeland College, in Alberta, Canada. Working out of her home, Jean prepared a dinner for more than 1,000 people, which launched a flourishing catering operation that continued for over 18 years. During that time, she had countless opportunities to test new ideas with immediate feedback—resulting in empty plates and contented customers! Whether preparing cocktail sandwiches for a house party or serving a hot meal for 1,500 people, Jean Paré earned a reputation for good food, courteous service and reasonable prices.

As requests for her recipes mounted, Jean was often asked the question, "Why don't you write a cookbook?" Jean responded by teaming up with her son, Grant Lovig, in the fall of 1980 to form Company's Coming Publishing Limited. The publication of *150 Delicious Squares* on April 14, 1981 marked the debut of what would soon become one of the world's most popular cookbook series.

The company has grown since those early days when Jean worked from a spare bedroom in her home. Today, she continues to write recipes while working closely with the staff of the Recipe Factory, as the Company's Coming test kitchen is affectionately known. There she fills the role of mentor, assisting with the development of recipes people most want to use for everyday cooking and easy entertaining. Every Company's Coming recipe is *kitchen-tested* before it's approved for publication.

Jean's daughter, Gail Lovig, is responsible for marketing and distribution, leading a team that includes sales personnel located in major cities across Canada. In addition, Company's Coming cookbooks are published and distributed under licence in the United States, Australia and other world markets. Bestsellers many times over in English, Company's Coming cookbooks have also been published in French and Spanish.

Familiar and trusted in home kitchens around the world, Company's Coming cookbooks are offered in a variety of formats. Highly regarded as kitchen workbooks, the softcover Original Series, with its lay-flat plastic comb binding, is still a favourite among readers.

Jean Paré's approach to cooking has always called for *quick and easy recipes* using *everyday ingredients.* That view has served her well. The recipient of many awards, including the Queen Elizabeth Golden Jubilee medal, Jean was appointed a Member of the Order of Canada, her country's highest lifetime achievement honour.

Jean continues to gain new supporters by adhering to what she calls The Golden Rule of Cooking: *"Never share a recipe you wouldn't use yourself."* It's an approach that works—*millions of times over!*

Foreword

Hectic school days can keep you hopping, but don't let a busy schedule prevent you from making a balanced, tasty lunch for your kids. With a little planning, and help from *School Days Lunches,* you can provide a nutritious homemade lunch, plus spend quality time with your children in the kitchen.

Lunchtime isn't just for munching sandwiches at home or at school. Make a delicious hot or cold wrap, or create something from last night's leftovers. Pack kid-size portions of salad, soup, chili or stew, or cut up fruit or vegetables along with a tasty dipping sauce. See our helpful "Just For Fun" tips, page 8, for making lunchtime appealing and fun for your little ones. Keep school lunches fresh by following our Food Safety Tips, page 9.

Studies have shown that children who help make their own lunch are more likely to eat it. So, with each recipe we've included "Kids Can Help" ideas. This is a great opportunity to introduce your children to chopping and slicing, stirring and spreading, grating and rolling, washing and tossing. You can have them open cans, count items, measure amounts and, of course, crack open an egg! Teaching your children kitchen skills in their elementary years creates an excellent foundation for developing good cooking skills, as well as nutrition awareness for their future years.

A nutritious lunch complements an active, healthy lifestyle—habits that last children a lifetime. So, whether having lunch at home or taking it to school, make lunchtime deliciously fun with *School Days Lunches.*

Nutrition Information Guidelines

Each recipe is analyzed using the most current version of the Canadian Nutrient File from Health Canada, which is based on the United States Department of Agriculture (USDA) Nutrient Database.

- If more than one ingredient is listed (such as "hard margarine or butter"), or if a range is given (1 – 2 tsp., 5 – 10 mL), only the first ingredient or first amount is analyzed.

- For meat, poultry and fish, the serving size per person is based on the recommended 4 oz. (113 g) uncooked weight (without bone), which is 2 – 3 oz. (57 – 85 g) cooked weight (without bone)—approximately the size of a deck of playing cards.

- Milk used is 1% M.F. (milk fat), unless otherwise stated.

- Cooking oil used is canola oil, unless otherwise stated.

- Ingredients indicating "sprinkle," "optional," or "for garnish" are not included in the nutrition information.

Margaret Ng, B.Sc. (Hon.), M.A.
Registered Dietitian

Just For Fun

Want help to make lunchtime exciting and fun for your kids?
Here are some tips to do just that!

For a visual treat, layer various colours of fruit or vegetables in clear bags or containers so they can see all the fresh goodness they'll be enjoying.

Make affordable and nutritious lunchtime combos that will keep kids interested in lunch without the extra sugar and fat in the commercial combos. It's better for the kids—and your pocketbook! Kids are less likely to buy junk food if they have a healthy and tasty alternative such as fruit cut into slices, vegetable sticks and dips, homemade muffins and healthy cookies.

Prepare their favourite foods in miniature. Cut sandwiches, vegetables, fruit and snacks into bite-size pieces. Kids love it when the food they eat fits easily into their hands and mouths.

Create theme lunches like Mexican Monday, Treats Tuesday or Whatever-You-Wish Wednesday! Keep their taste buds on their toes.

Rejuvenate their favourite standbys by cutting sandwiches with cookie cutters shaped like stars, circles or squares. Or forget the bread and try using a pita or tortilla stuffed with their favourite fillings.

Roll lunch meats with filling into sushi and secure with wooden picks.

Encourage kids to drink lots of water or healthier drink alternatives like milk or natural fruit juices instead of sugary, caffeinated beverages. If water seems too boring for them, add a couple drops of fresh lime, lemon or citrus flavour. Soon they'll know how thirst-quenching water can be.

Take your kids to the grocery store and show them all the healthy foods available. Let them choose snacks and the occasional treat, making them a partner in the lunch-making process. Kids will also enjoy flipping through the full-colour photos in *School Days Lunches* while deciding what they'd like for tomorrow's lunch, whether at home or at school.

This book is intended for adults to use. But because we are encouraging you to have your children help, please supervise them as necessary. Younger children especially need careful monitoring with the handling of sharp knives, hot or boiling liquids and other tools such as graters that could cause them harm.

Food Safety Tips
(for you and your child)

- Always wash your hands before and after you make lunch.

- Remember to occasionally wash your lunch box or bag.

- Wash all fruits and vegetables before preparing or eating them.

- Don't use meat, poultry, seafood, eggs, mayonnaise or dairy products if you can't keep them cool.

- Use freezer packs or frozen juice boxes to keep lunch cold. Food should stay at 40°F (4°C).

- Keep lunch boxes and bags out of the sun and away from heat sources.

- Hot foods must stay hot to be safe to eat. Keep at 140°F (60°C).

- Before adding food to an insulated container, preheat it using hot water or chill it with cold.

- To avoid confusion, label the foods in each child's lunch so they know what they're eating and what goes with what.

- Wrap lettuce, tomatoes, carrot sticks and pickles separately from sandwiches or wraps to keep the bread or tortilla from becoming soggy.

- Pack salad dressing or dipping sauce in small resealable plastic containers.

- Pack foods snugly so they won't move around in lunch boxes or bags.

- Keep snacks portable by cutting them into bite-size pieces.

- Put pre-moistened wipes in their lunch to clean hands before and after lunch, or add a paper towel or napkin.

In consideration of children who have allergies to nuts, all of the recipes in this book are nut-free.

Hot Apple Cider

Who wouldn't love to walk in the door to the wonderful aroma of apple, cinnamon and cloves! Serve it to kids while they do their homework. A perfect thermos filler to take to school on cold days.

Apple juice	2 cups	500 mL
Strip of orange peel (about 2 inches, 5 cm)	1	1
Cinnamon stick (4 inches, 10 cm)	1	1
Whole cloves	3	3

Combine all 4 ingredients in medium saucepan. Bring to a boil on medium-high. Reduce heat to medium-low. Cover. Simmer for about 15 minutes until fragrant. Strain through sieve into 4 cup (1 L) liquid measure. Discard solids. Makes about 1 2/3 cups (400 mL). Serves 2.

1 serving: 123 Calories; 0.3 g Total Fat (0 g Mono, 0.1 g Poly, 0.1 g Sat); 0 mg Cholesterol; 31 g Carbohydrate; trace Fibre; 0 g Protein; 8 mg Sodium

Pictured on page 11.

Kids Can Help

Counting out cloves. Pouring juice into saucepan.

Vanilla Hot Chocolate

Hot and frothy, with a splash of smooth vanilla flavour. Garnish with coloured marshmallows just for fun! To take to school, pour hot drink into a warm thermos and put some marshmallows into a plastic bag.

Chocolate milk	1 cup	250 mL
Vanilla-flavoured syrup (such as Torani's)	2 – 3 tsp.	10 – 15 mL

Measure both ingredients into microwave-safe mug. Stir. Microwave on high (100%) for 1 to 2 minutes until hot. Stir. Cool slightly. Makes about 1 cup (250 mL). Serves 1.

1 serving: 228 Calories; 5.3 g Total Fat (1.6 g Mono, 0.2 g Poly, 3.3 g Sat); 18 mg Cholesterol; 38 g Carbohydrate; 2 g Fibre; 8 g Protein; 176 mg Sodium

Pictured on page 11.

(continued on next page)

RASPBERRY HOT CHOCOLATE: Omit vanilla-flavoured syrup. Use same amount of raspberry-flavoured syrup (such as Torani's).

Kids Can Help

Measuring ingredients. Stirring. Setting time on microwave.

Left: Vanilla Hot Chocolate, page 10
Right: Hot Apple Cider, page 10

Iced Apple Tea

An exciting combination of flavours will make this a summertime favourite with kids of all ages. Pour into a chilled thermos for school.

Cranberry cocktail, approximately	1 1/2 cups	375 mL
Apple juice	4 cups	1 L
Cold water	3 cups	750 mL
Powdered iced tea mix, with lemon	1/3 cup	75 mL

Pour cranberry cocktail into ice cube tray. Freeze until firm.

Measure remaining 3 ingredients into large pitcher. Stir until iced tea mix is dissolved. Add cranberry cocktail cubes. Stir. Makes about 9 cups (2.25 L). Serves 9.

1 serving: 119 Calories; 0.2 g Total Fat (0 g Mono, 0.1 g Poly, 0 g Sat); 0 mg Cholesterol; 30 g Carbohydrate; trace Fibre; 0 g Protein; 5 mg Sodium

Pictured on back cover.

Kids Can Help

Measuring ingredients. Stirring.

Orange Iced Tea

Light orange flavour in a refreshing iced tea—sure to cool kids down on a warm school day.

Boiling water	4 cups	1 L
Orange pekoe tea bags	2	2
Orange juice	1 cup	250 mL
Granulated sugar	3 – 4 tbsp.	50 – 60 mL
Ice cubes		

Pour boiling water into large heatproof pitcher or 8 cup (2 L) liquid measure. Add tea bags. Cover. Let steep for 5 minutes. Squeeze and discard tea bags.

(continued on next page)

Add orange juice and sugar. Stir until sugar is dissolved. Chill for 3 to 4 hours until cold. Makes about 5 cups (1.25 L).

Pour over ice cubes in 5 medium glasses. To take to school, pour into chilled thermos. Serves 5.

1 serving: 56 Calories; 0.1 g Total Fat (0 g Mono, 0 g Poly, 0 g Sat); 0 mg Cholesterol; 14 g Carbohydrate; trace Fibre; 0 g Protein; 8 mg Sodium

Pictured above.

Kids Can Help

Measuring sugar. Stirring. Putting ice cubes into individual glasses.

Fruity Shake-Up

A great breakfast smoothie. Using chilled apple juice and frozen strawberries will make this a thicker beverage. Take it to school in a chilled thermos. Don't forget to shake it before drinking.

Raisins	2 tbsp.	30 mL
Apple juice	1/4 cup	60 mL
Frozen ripe medium banana, cut up (see Tip, page 16)	1	1
Apple juice	3/4 cup	175 mL
Sliced fresh (or 2 – 3 frozen whole) strawberries	1/2 cup	125 mL
Lemon juice	1/2 tsp.	2 mL

Process raisins and first amount of apple juice in blender for about 1 minute, scraping down sides if necessary, until almost smooth.

Add remaining 4 ingredients. Process until smooth. Makes about 2 cups (500 mL). Serves 2.

1 serving: 156 Calories; 0.6 g Total Fat (0.1 g Mono, 0.2 g Poly, 0.2 g Sat); 0 mg Cholesterol; 39 g Carbohydrate; 2 g Fibre; 1 g Protein; 6 mg Sodium

Pictured on page 17.

Kids Can Help

Measuring raisins. Washing fresh strawberries. Putting ingredients into blender and turning blender on and off.

Very Berry

Beautiful, bright red colour with a berry sweet, berry refreshing flavour.

Fresh (or frozen whole) strawberries	6	6
Cranberry cocktail	1/2 cup	125 mL
Raspberry sherbet	1/4 cup	60 mL
Liquid honey	1 – 2 tsp.	5 – 10 mL

(continued on next page)

Process all 4 ingredients in blender until smooth. Makes about 1 1/2 cups (375 mL). Serves 2.

1 serving: 100 Calories; 0.8 g Total Fat (0.2 g Mono, 0.1 g Poly, 0.3 g Sat); 1 mg Cholesterol; 24 g Carbohydrate; 1 g Fibre; 1 g Protein; 14 mg Sodium

Pictured below.

Kids Can Help

Counting and washing fresh strawberries. Putting ingredients into blender and turning blender on and off.

Tropical Hurricane

Frothy bubbles top this creamy, pale yellow drink. Pour into chilled thermos and take to school. Shake gently before drinking.

Can of light coconut milk	14 oz.	398 mL
Can of pineapple tidbits (with juice)	8 oz.	227 mL
Frozen ripe medium banana, cut up (see Tip, below)	1	1
Apricot nectar	1/4 cup	60 mL

Shake can of coconut milk well. Pour into ice cube tray. Freeze until firm.

Put remaining 3 ingredients into blender. Add 6 coconut milk cubes (see Note). Process until smooth. Makes about 2 1/3 cups (575 mL). Serves 2.

1 serving: 332 Calories; 18.2 g Total Fat (0.1 g Mono, 0.1 g Poly, 15.9 g Sat); 0 mg Cholesterol; 42 g Carbohydrate; 2 g Fibre; 5 g Protein; 27 mg Sodium

Pictured on page 17.

Kids Can Help

Transferring frozen cubes to resealable freezer bag for storage.
Putting ingredients into blender and turning blender on and off.

Note: Store extra frozen coconut milk cubes in resealable freezer bag for the next time you make this drink or to use in other smoothie recipes.

Tip: To use overripe bananas, peel and cut them into 2 inch (5 cm) pieces. Arrange in single layer in ungreased 9 x 13 inch (22 x 33 cm) pan. Freeze until firm. Store in resealable freezer bag. Use 4 pieces for 1 medium banana. Overripe bananas provide rich flavour to beverages.

Left: Fruity Shake-Up, page 14
Right: Tropical Hurricane, above

Choco-Berry Shake

Chocolate-covered strawberries—in a glass. Delightful!
Take it to school in a chilled thermos. Shake gently and drink up.

Milk	1 cup	250 mL
Strawberry ice cream	1/4 cup	60 mL
Chocolate syrup	2 – 3 tbsp.	30 – 50 mL
Fresh (or frozen whole) strawberries	6	6
Ice cubes	4	4

Process all 5 ingredients in blender until smooth. Makes about 3 cups (750 mL). Serves 3.

1 serving: 117 Calories; 3.9 g Total Fat (0.8 g Mono, 0.6 g Poly, 1.4 g Sat); 9 mg Cholesterol; 18 g Carbohydrate; 1 g Fibre; 4 g Protein; 69 mg Sodium

Pictured on page 19.

Kids Can Help

Washing fresh strawberries. Counting strawberries and ice cubes. Putting ingredients into blender and turning blender on and off.

Banana Pick-Me-Up

A quick, nutritious lunch or after-school energizer for kids on the go. Thick and creamy, with a mild chocolate flavour. Pour into a chilled thermos and take it to school. Shake before drinking.

Frozen ripe medium bananas, cut up (see Tip, page 16)	2	2
Milk	1 cup	250 mL
Diced soft tofu	1/2 cup	125 mL
Plain yogurt	1/2 cup	125 mL
Instant chocolate drink powder	2 tbsp.	30 mL
Wheat germ	1 tbsp.	15 mL

Process all 6 ingredients in blender until smooth. Makes about 3 1/4 cups (800 mL). Serves 3.

(continued on next page)

1 serving: *226 Calories; 4.7 g Total Fat (1.1 g Mono, 1.5 g Poly, 1.8 g Sat); 6 mg Cholesterol; 40 g Carbohydrate; 2 g Fibre; 10 g Protein; 108 mg Sodium*

Pictured below.

Variation: Add 2 tbsp. (30 mL) malt drink mix (such as Ovaltine) to ingredients in blender. Process until smooth.

Kids Can Help

Putting ingredients into blender and turning blender on and off.

Top Left: Banana Pick-Me-Up, page 18   Bottom Right: Choco-Berry Shake, page 18

Orange Melon Salad

Creamy caramel coats cool cantaloupe. Watermelon and marshmallows add to the mix. Keep chilled if taking to school.

Medium orange, peeled, cut up	1	1
Cubed cantaloupe	1/2 cup	125 mL
Cubed seedless watermelon	1/2 cup	125 mL
Miniature marshmallows	16	16
Caramel ice cream topping	1 tbsp.	15 mL

Put first 4 ingredients into medium bowl. Toss. Drizzle with ice cream topping. Toss gently. May be stored in airtight container in refrigerator for up to 2 days. Makes about 1 3/4 cups (425 mL).

1/2 cup (125 mL): 62 Calories; 0.2 g Total Fat (0 g Mono, 0 g Poly, 0 g Sat); 0 mg Cholesterol; 15 g Carbohydrate; 1 g Fibre; 1 g Protein; 25 mg Sodium

Pictured on page 21.

Kids Can Help

Peeling orange. Counting marshmallows.

Apple Raisin Salad

Apples, pineapple and a dash of spice make this a tasty, light lunch or a perfect side dish. Serve on a lettuce leaf at home or pack individual servings in plastic containers for school. Keep chilled.

Medium cooking apples (such as McIntosh), with peel, cores removed, diced	2	2
Tart medium cooking apple (such as Granny Smith), with peel, core removed, diced	1	1
Can of pineapple tidbits, drained and juice reserved	8 oz.	227 mL
Reserved pineapple juice	1 tbsp.	15 mL

(continued on next page)

2% cottage cheese	1 cup	250 mL
Dark raisins	1/2 cup	125 mL
Ground cinnamon	1/4 tsp.	1 mL

Put first 4 ingredients into large bowl. Toss until apple is coated with pineapple juice.

Add remaining 3 ingredients. Stir well. May be stored in airtight container in refrigerator for up to 2 days. Makes about 5 cups (1.25 L).

1 cup (250 mL): 156 Calories; 2.4 g Total Fat (0.6 g Mono, 0.2 g Poly, 1.3 g Sat); 7 mg Cholesterol; 30 g Carbohydrate; 3 g Fibre; 6 g Protein; 182 mg Sodium

Pictured below.

Kids Can Help

Washing apples. Measuring raisins. Stirring.

Top Right: Apple Raisin Salad, page 20
Left and Bottom Right: Orange Melon Salad, page 20

Spinach Fruit Salad

A colourful addition to any meal. Use a small scoop to make cantaloupe balls for something a little fancier. Kids will have fun helping use the scoop!

SWEET AND TANGY DRESSING

White (or apple cider) vinegar	1 1/2 tbsp.	25 mL
Granulated sugar	1 1/2 tbsp.	25 mL
Cooking oil	1 tbsp.	15 mL
Salt, sprinkle		
Fresh spinach, stems removed, lightly packed	1 cup	250 mL
Cantaloupe balls	1/3 cup	75 mL
Fresh strawberries, quartered	1/4 cup	60 mL
Shelled pumpkin seeds (optional)	2 tbsp.	30 mL

Sweet And Tangy Dressing: Measure first 4 ingredients into small cup. Stir until sugar is dissolved. Makes about 1/4 cup (60 mL) dressing.

Put remaining 4 ingredients into medium bowl. Toss gently. Drizzle with dressing. Toss gently. Makes about 2 cups (500 mL).

1 cup (250 mL): 122 Calories; 7.2 g Total Fat (4.1 g Mono, 2.1 g Poly, 0.5 g Sat); 0 mg Cholesterol; 15 g Carbohydrate; 1 g Fibre; 1 g Protein; 26 mg Sodium

Pictured on front cover.

LETTUCE FRUIT SALAD: Omit spinach. Use same amount of chopped or torn romaine lettuce.

Kids Can Help

Stirring dressing. Removing spinach stems. Washing and cutting strawberries. Measuring pumpkin seeds.

Elbows-On-The-Table Salad

Quick and easy, mild and creamy. Kids will love the colourful vegetables and elbow macaroni coated in a simple, but delicious dressing. Serve this with chicken drumsticks and tell them it's all "arms and legs" for lunch!

FASTA PASTA DRESSING

Salad dressing (or mayonnaise)	2 tbsp.	30 mL
Sour cream	1 tbsp.	15 mL
Prepared mustard	1 tsp.	5 mL
Cooked elbow macaroni (about 2/3 cup, 150 mL, uncooked)	1 cup	250 mL
Chopped celery	1/4 cup	60 mL
Grated carrot	1/4 cup	60 mL
Grated medium Cheddar cheese	1/4 cup	60 mL
Sliced green onion	1 – 2 tbsp.	15 – 30 mL

Fasta Pasta Dressing: Combine first 3 ingredients in small cup. Makes 3 tbsp. (50 mL) dressing.

Put remaining 5 ingredients into medium bowl. Toss. Drizzle with dressing. Toss well. Cover. Chill for 2 hours to blend flavours. May be stored in airtight container in refrigerator for up to 2 days. Makes about 2 cups (500 mL).

1 cup (250 mL): 262 Calories; 14 g Total Fat (5.9 g Mono, 3 g Poly, 4.4 g Sat); 23 mg Cholesterol; 26 g Carbohydrate; 2 g Fibre; 8 g Protein; 249 mg Sodium

Pictured on page 25.

Kids Can Help

Measuring and stirring dressing ingredients. Washing vegetables. Peeling and grating carrot. Grating cheese. Tossing salad.

Spiral Ham Salad

Spirals of pasta and ribbons of ham are perfectly paired with creamy honey mustard dressing. Pack in an airtight container to take to school. Keep chilled.

HONEY MUSTARD DRESSING

Mayonnaise	2/3 cup	150 mL
Liquid honey	1 tsp.	5 mL
Prepared mustard	1 tsp.	5 mL
Cooked rotini (or other spiral) pasta (about 1 1/2 cups, 375 mL, uncooked)	2 cups	500 mL
Thinly sliced deli ham, cut into strips	1/2 cup	125 mL
Chopped celery	1/2 cup	125 mL
Frozen peas, thawed	1/2 cup	125 mL
Chopped sweet pickle (or 2 tbsp., 30 mL, sweet pickle relish)	1/4 cup	60 mL
Chopped onion (optional)	1/4 cup	60 mL
Medium tomato, chopped	1	1

Honey Mustard Dressing: Combine first 3 ingredients in small bowl. Makes about 2/3 cup (150 mL) dressing.

Put next 6 ingredients into large bowl. Toss. Drizzle with dressing. Toss well.

Scatter tomato over top. May be stored in airtight container in refrigerator for up to 2 days. Makes about 4 cups (1 L).

1 cup (250 mL): 471 Calories; 34 g Total Fat (18.4 g Mono, 11 g Poly, 3.7 g Sat); 34 mg Cholesterol; 33 g Carbohydrate; 2 g Fibre; 9 g Protein; 638 mg Sodium

Pictured on page 25.

Kids Can Help

Stirring dressing. Tossing salad. Scattering tomato.

Top: Elbows-On-The-Table Salad, page 23
Bottom: Spiral Ham Salad, above

Crunchy Jelly Salad

*A great way to get kids to eat their vegetables—subtly disguised
in gelatin just bursting with tangy orange flavour!*

Can of mandarin orange segments (with juice)	10 oz.	284 mL
Boiling water	2/3 cup	150 mL
Box of orange-flavoured jelly powder (gelatin)	3 oz.	85 g
Envelope of unflavoured gelatin (1 tbsp., 15 mL)	1	1
Salt	1/8 tsp.	0.5 mL
Orange juice	1 1/3 cups	325 mL
Lemon juice	1 tbsp.	15 mL
Finely chopped cabbage	1/2 cup	125 mL
Grated carrot	1/3 cup	75 mL
Grated zucchini (with peel)	1/4 cup	60 mL

Drain juice from mandarin orange segments into medium bowl. Set orange segments aside.

Add boiling water to mandarin orange juice. Stir. Add next 3 ingredients. Stir until gelatin is dissolved.

Add orange juice and lemon juice. Stir. Chill for about 40 minutes, stirring occasionally, until partially thickened.

Add reserved orange segments and remaining 3 ingredients to gelatin mixture. Stir gently. Cover. Chill for about 2 hours until set. May be stored in airtight container in refrigerator for up to 2 days. Makes about 4 cups (1 L).

1/2 cup (125 mL): 84 Calories; 0.1 g Total Fat (0 g Mono, 0 g Poly, 0 g Sat); 0 mg Cholesterol; 19 g Carbohydrate; trace Fibre; 3 g Protein; 74 mg Sodium

Pictured on page 27.

Kids Can Help

Stirring gelatin. Measuring juices. Grating carrot and zucchini.

Top: Mixed Cup Salad, page 28
Bottom: Crunchy Jelly Salad, above

Salads

Mixed Cup Salad

Cupfuls of colour make rice extra nice! Everyone is sure to love this easy-to-make luncheon salad coated with dilly-icious dressing.

DILL DRESSING

Plain yogurt	1 cup	250 mL
French dressing	1/4 cup	60 mL
Chopped fresh dill (or 1/2 tsp., 2 mL, dill weed)	2 tsp.	10 mL
Cooked rice (2/3 cup, 150 mL, uncooked)	2 cups	500 mL
Frozen kernel corn, thawed	1 cup	250 mL
Diced English cucumber (with peel)	1 cup	250 mL
Diced red pepper	1 cup	250 mL
Grated carrot	1 cup	250 mL
Diced cooked ham	1 cup	250 mL
Diced medium Cheddar cheese	1 cup	250 mL

Dill Dressing: Combine first 3 ingredients in small bowl. Cover. Let stand for 10 minutes to blend flavours. Makes about 1 1/4 cups (300 mL) dressing.

Put remaining 7 ingredients into large bowl. Toss gently. Drizzle with dressing. Toss gently. May be stored in airtight container in refrigerator for up to 2 days. Makes about 8 cups (2 L).

1 cup (250 mL): 333 Calories; 14.4 g Total Fat (5.7 g Mono, 2.2 g Poly, 5.8 g Sat); 44 mg Cholesterol; 35 g Carbohydrate; 2 g Fibre; 16 g Protein; 710 mg Sodium

Pictured on page 27.

Kids Can Help

Stirring dressing. Washing vegetables. Peeling and grating carrot. Tossing salad.

Oriental Chicken Slaw

Make this for the next day's lunches when you have leftover roast chicken.
Delicious served on rice.

SWEET AND SOUR DRESSING

Cooking oil	2 tbsp.	30 mL
Liquid honey	4 tsp.	20 mL
White vinegar	4 tsp.	20 mL
Soy sauce	2 tsp.	10 mL
Shredded cabbage, lightly packed	1 cup	250 mL
Grated carrot	1/2 cup	125 mL
Chopped cooked chicken	1/2 cup	125 mL
Chopped green pepper	1/4 cup	60 mL
Chopped red onion	2 tbsp.	30 mL
Oriental steam-fried noodles, broken up	2/3 cup	150 mL

Sweet And Sour Dressing: Combine first 4 ingredients in jar with tight-fitting lid. Shake well. Makes about 1/3 cup (75 mL) dressing.

Put next 5 ingredients into medium bowl. Toss. Drizzle with dressing. Toss well.

Just before serving, scatter noodles over top. May be stored in airtight container in refrigerator for up to 2 days. Makes about 3 cups (750 mL).

1 cup (250 mL): 221 Calories; 11.6 g Total Fat (6.2 g Mono, 3.3 g Poly, 1.3 g Sat); 31 mg Cholesterol; 21 g Carbohydrate; 1 g Fibre; 10 g Protein; 268 mg Sodium

Pictured on page 31.

Kids Can Help

Washing vegetables. Peeling and grating carrot. Shaking dressing.

Taco Chip Salad

Round up the kids! Cheesy orange tortilla chips brighten this southwestern-style salad they're sure to love. Ready in just minutes!

BACK-AT-THE-RANCH DRESSING

Ranch-style dressing	2 tbsp.	30 mL
Ketchup	1 tbsp.	15 mL
Chopped green onion	1 tbsp.	15 mL
Chopped or torn romaine lettuce, lightly packed	1 cup	250 mL
Chopped tomato	1/2 cup	125 mL
Sliced English cucumber (with peel)	1/4 cup	60 mL
Chopped red pepper	1/4 cup	60 mL
Grated medium Cheddar cheese	1/4 cup	60 mL
Cheese-flavoured tortilla chips	1 cup	250 mL

Back-At-The-Ranch Dressing: Combine first 3 ingredients in small cup. Makes about 1/4 cup (60 mL) dressing.

Put next 5 ingredients into medium bowl. Toss. Drizzle with dressing. Toss well. Makes about 2 cups (500 mL) salad.

Serve with tortilla chips. Serves 2.

1 serving: 162 Calories; 10.3 g Total Fat (2.1 g Mono, 0.6 g Poly, 2 g Sat); 3 mg Cholesterol; 16 g Carbohydrate; 2 g Fibre; 3 g Protein; 379 mg Sodium

Pictured on page 31.

Kids Can Help

Stirring dressing. Washing vegetables. Preparing lettuce.
Grating cheese. Tossing salad.

Top: Oriental Chicken Slaw, page 29
Bottom: Taco Chip Salad, above

Salmon Croissant

Rich salmon filling on a delicate croissant. Delicious with a salad or fresh fruit.
Add a glass of Orange Iced Tea, page 12.

SALMON SALAD FILLING

Canned salmon, drained, skin and round bones removed, flaked	1/3 cup	75 mL
Finely chopped red pepper	2 tbsp.	30 mL
Salad dressing (or mayonnaise)	1 tbsp.	15 mL
Finely chopped green onion (optional)	1 tbsp.	15 mL
Lemon juice	1 tsp.	5 mL
Salt, sprinkle		
Pepper, sprinkle		
Croissant, split	1	1

Salmon Salad Filling: Combine first 7 ingredients in small bowl. Makes about 1/2 cup (125 mL) filling.

Spread filling evenly on bottom half of croissant. Cover with top half. Makes 1 salmon croissant.

1 salmon croissant: 430 Calories; 24.9 g Total Fat (9 g Mono, 4.7 g Poly, 8.9 g Sat); 84 mg Cholesterol; 34 g Carbohydrate; 2 g Fibre; 17 g Protein; 616 mg Sodium

Pictured on page 33.

Kids Can Help

Stirring and spreading filling.

Salami Cheese Sub

This sub will rise to the top of your children's list of favourite lunches!
Try with other cold cuts for variety.

Ketchup	1 tbsp.	15 mL
Salad dressing (or mayonnaise)	1 tbsp.	15 mL
Submarine bun (6 inch, 15 cm, size), split	1	1

(continued on next page)

Top: Salami Cheese Sub, page 32

Bottom: Salmon Croissant, page 32

Process cheese slice (your favourite), halved	1	1
Deli salami (about 3 slices)	1/2 oz.	14 g
Chopped or torn lettuce (your favourite), lightly packed	1/4 cup	60 mL

Combine ketchup and salad dressing in small cup. Divide and spread on both halves of bun.

Layer cheese, salami and lettuce on bottom half of bun. Cover with top half. Makes 1 sub.

1 sub: 471 Calories; 24.5 g Total Fat (10.4 g Mono, 3.8 g Poly, 8.9 g Sat); 44 mg Cholesterol; 45 g Carbohydrate; trace Fibre; 17 g Protein; 1437 mg Sodium

Pictured above.

Kids Can Help

Stirring. Tearing lettuce. Layering ingredients on bun.

Chicken Cheese Pitas

*Colourful and crunchy, this cheesy chicken salad is sure
to satisfy lunch-hour cravings. Serve with fresh veggies or fruit.*

CHEESY CHICKEN FILLING

Process cheese spread	1 – 2 tbsp.	15 – 30 mL
Mayonnaise	1 tbsp.	15 mL
Orange juice	1 tbsp.	15 mL
Chopped cooked chicken	1/2 cup	125 mL
Chopped celery	1/4 cup	60 mL
Chopped red pepper	1/4 cup	60 mL
Chopped green onion	1 – 2 tbsp.	15 – 30 mL
Salt, sprinkle		
Pepper, sprinkle		
Pita breads (3 inch, 7.5 cm, diameter)	4	4
Chopped or torn iceberg lettuce, lightly packed	1/2 – 1 cup	125 – 250 mL

Cheesy Chicken Filling: Combine first 3 ingredients in small cup.

Put next 6 ingredients into medium bowl. Toss well. Drizzle with cheese mixture. Toss gently. Makes about 1 1/3 cups (325 mL) filling.

Cut top off each pita 1/2 inch (1.2 cm) from edge. Discard tops. Open pockets. Divide and stuff lettuce into each pocket. Spoon about 1/3 cup (75 mL) filling into each. Makes 4 stuffed pitas.

1 stuffed pita: 121 Calories; 5.3 g Total Fat (2.3 g Mono, 1.4 g Poly, 1.2 g Sat); 21 mg Cholesterol; 10 g Carbohydrate; 1 g Fibre; 8 g Protein; 188 mg Sodium

Pictured on front cover.

Kids Can Help

Measuring ingredients. Tossing filling. Stuffing pitas.

Tip: To toast seeds and coconut, spread evenly in ungreased shallow pan. Bake in 350°F (175°C) oven for 5 to 10 minutes, stirring or shaking often, until desired doneness.

Bacon Salad Sandwich

If your kids like spinach salad, they'll love this scrumptious sandwich!
If preferred, leave bread untoasted. Serve with a glass of juice or milk.

Ranch-style dressing	4 tsp.	20 mL
Bread slices (your favourite), toasted	2	2
Fresh spinach leaves, stems removed	10 – 12	10 – 12
Large hard-cooked egg, sliced	1	1
Bacon slices, cooked crisp, broken into 3 pieces each	3	3

Divide and spread dressing on 1 side of each toast slice.

Arrange spinach on top of dressing on 1 slice. Layer egg slices and bacon pieces over top. Cover with remaining toast slice, dressing-side down. Press down lightly. To serve, cut in half or into quarters. Makes 1 sandwich.

1 sandwich: 417 Calories; 25.1 g Total Fat (7.2 g Mono, 2.2 g Poly, 7 g Sat); 235 mg Cholesterol; 29 g Carbohydrate; 1 g Fibre; 18 g Protein; 926 mg Sodium

Pictured below.

Kids Can Help

Toasting bread. Spreading dressing. Breaking up bacon. Layering ingredients.

Wrap 'N' Roll

For those who love Tex-Mex flavours. These are good to have on hand in the freezer for the days you need lunch in a hurry. Be sure to try the tasty variations, too. Send small containers of salsa and sour cream for dipping.

BEAN FILLING

Can of mixed beans, rinsed and drained	19 oz.	540 mL
Mild (or medium) salsa	1/4 cup	60 mL
Cream cheese, softened	1/4 cup	60 mL
Flour (or whole wheat flour) tortillas (9 inch, 22 cm, diameter)	8	8
Deli ham slices	8	8

Bean Filling: Mash beans with fork in medium bowl.

Add salsa and cream cheese. Stir well. Makes about 2 cups (500 mL) filling.

Spread about 1/4 cup (60 mL) filling evenly on 1 tortilla, almost to edge.

Place 1 ham slice on top of filling. Roll up tightly, jelly roll-style. Repeat with remaining filling, tortillas and ham, for a total of 8 wraps. Freezes well. To serve, cut each wrap in half diagonally. Makes 8 wraps.

1 wrap: 304 Calories; 10.5 g Total Fat (4.1 g Mono, 2.1 g Poly, 3.5 g Sat); 29 mg Cholesterol; 38 g Carbohydrate; 3 g Fibre; 14 g Protein; 836 mg Sodium

CHEESY WRAP 'N' ROLL: Sprinkle 2 tbsp. (30 mL) grated medium (or mild) Cheddar cheese on top of bean filling on each tortilla before adding ham.

Pictured on page 37.

VEGGIE WRAP 'N' ROLL: Omit ham. Sprinkle 2 tbsp. (30 mL) grated carrot on top of bean filling on each tortilla before rolling.

Kids Can Help

Mashing beans. Stirring filling. Rolling tortillas.

Top: Crunchy Ham Pockets, page 38
Bottom: Cheesy Wrap 'N' Roll, above

Cold Sandwiches & Wraps

Crunchy Ham Pockets

Crunchy pickle, vegetables, ham and a cool dill dressing fill pita pockets perfectly!

CRUNCHY HAM FILLING

Chopped cooked ham	1 cup	250 mL
Finely chopped celery	1/4 cup	60 mL
Finely chopped red (or green) pepper	1/4 cup	60 mL
Sour cream	2 tbsp.	30 mL
Salad dressing (or mayonnaise)	2 tbsp.	30 mL
Chopped green onion	1 tbsp.	15 mL
Chopped dill pickle	1 tbsp.	15 mL
Dill weed	1/4 tsp.	1 mL
Chopped or torn lettuce (your favourite), lightly packed	1/2 – 1 cup	125 – 250 mL
Pita breads (8 inch, 20 cm, diameter), halved crosswise	2	2

Crunchy Ham Filling: Combine first 8 ingredients in small bowl. Makes about 1 1/3 cups (325 mL) filling.

Divide and stuff lettuce into each pita pocket. Spoon about 1/3 cup (75 mL) ham filling into each. Makes 4 stuffed pockets.

1 stuffed pocket: 213 Calories; 8.3 g Total Fat (3.8 g Mono, 1.8 g Poly, 2 g Sat); 24 mg Cholesterol; 24 g Carbohydrate; 1 g Fibre; 11 g Protein; 781 mg Sodium

Pictured on page 37.

Kids Can Help

Stirring filling. Stuffing pita pockets.

Beefy Roll-Up

A great way to use leftover roast beef. A little corn relish adds a touch of sweetness. Dip in mustard or barbecue sauce.

CORN AND BEEF FILLING

Deli roast beef slices (or cooked roast beef), cut into thin strips	4 oz.	113 g
Corn relish	2 1/2 tbsp.	37 mL
Salad dressing (or mayonnaise)	1 tbsp.	15 mL
Flour tortilla (9 inch, 22 cm, diameter)	1	1

Corn And Beef Filling: Combine first 3 ingredients in small bowl. Makes about 1/2 cup (125 mL) filling.

Spread filling evenly on tortilla, almost to edge. Roll up tightly, jelly roll-style. To serve, cut in half diagonally. Makes 1 wrap.

1 wrap: 472 Calories; 17.2 g Total Fat (8 g Mono, 4.2 g Poly, 3.2 g Sat); 78 mg Cholesterol; 40 g Carbohydrate; 2 g Fibre; 40 g Protein; 595 mg Sodium

Pictured below.

Variation: Place green leaf lettuce on tortilla before filling and rolling.

Kids Can Help

Stirring filling. Rolling up tortilla.

Pizza Wedges

Looks like a cake—tastes like a pizza! Versatile and delicious.
Serve with sour cream, pizza sauce or Avocado Ranch Dip, page 108.
Can also be cut into slices to use instead of bread for spicy sandwiches.

Cooking oil	1 tbsp.	15 mL
Chopped onion	1 cup	250 mL
Garlic clove, minced (or 1/4 tsp., 1 mL, powder)	1	1
Paprika	2 tsp.	10 mL
Pepper	1/2 tsp.	2 mL
Chopped deli pepperoni slices	3/4 cup	175 mL
All-purpose flour	1 1/2 cups	375 mL
Baking powder	2 tsp.	10 mL
Salt	1/4 tsp.	1 mL
Large eggs, fork-beaten	4	4
Grated Parmesan cheese	3/4 cup	175 mL
Tomato sauce	1/2 cup	125 mL
Hard margarine (or butter), melted	1/3 cup	75 mL
Chopped fresh oregano leaves (or 3/4 tsp., 4 mL, dried)	1 tbsp.	15 mL

Heat cooking oil in medium frying pan on medium. Add onion. Cook for 5 to 10 minutes, stirring often, until softened.

Add garlic, paprika and pepper. Heat and stir for 1 to 2 minutes until fragrant.

Add pepperoni. Heat and stir for about 5 minutes until pepperoni is lightly browned. Transfer mixture to small bowl. Cool.

Combine flour, baking powder and salt in large bowl. Make a well in centre.

Add pepperoni mixture and remaining 5 ingredients to well. Stir until just moistened. Spread evenly in greased 9 inch (22 cm) round pan. Bake in 375°F (190°C) oven for about 20 minutes until golden and wooden pick inserted in centre comes out clean. Let stand in pan for 5 minutes before removing to wire rack to cool. Freezes well. Cuts into 8 wedges.

1 wedge: 346 Calories; 21.8 g Total Fat (11.1 g Mono, 2.5 g Poly, 6.8 g Sat); 127 mg Cholesterol; 24 g Carbohydrate; 1 g Fibre; 13 g Protein; 863 mg Sodium

Pictured on page 41.

(continued on next page)

PIZZA MUFFINS: Grease 8 muffin cups with cooking spray. Fill cups almost full. Bake in 350°F (175°C) oven for about 20 minutes until wooden pick inserted in centre of muffin comes out clean. Let stand in pan for 5 minutes before removing to wire rack to cool. Makes 8 muffins.

Pictured below.

Kids Can Help

Measuring dry ingredients. Beating eggs. Stirring.

Top: Pizza Muffins, above
Bottom: Pizza Wedges, page 40

Speckled Spirals

These tasty rolls will remind you of quesadillas. Kids will like these hot or cold.

SOUTHWESTERN CHICKEN FILLING

Block of cream cheese, softened	4 oz.	125 g
Finely chopped cooked chicken	1/2 cup	125 mL
Grated Monterey Jack cheese	1/2 cup	125 mL
Finely chopped red pepper	2 tbsp.	30 mL
Finely chopped green pepper	2 tbsp.	30 mL
Chopped fresh parsley (or 1/2 tsp., 2 mL, flakes)	2 tsp.	10 mL
Chili powder	1 tsp.	5 mL
Salt	1/8 tsp.	0.5 mL
Flour tortillas (9 inch, 22 cm, diameter)	2	2

Southwestern Chicken Filling: Combine first 8 ingredients in medium bowl. Makes about 2 cups (500 mL) filling.

Spread about 1 cup (250 mL) filling evenly on 1 tortilla, almost to edge. Roll up tightly, jelly roll-style. Repeat with remaining filling and tortilla. Wrap rolls with plastic wrap. Chill for 2 hours. Discard plastic wrap. Trim about 1/2 inch (12 mm) from both ends of each roll. Cut each roll into 1/2 inch (12 mm) slices, for a total of about 32 slices. Serves 4.

1 serving: 291 Calories; 18.8 g Total Fat (5.7 g Mono, 1.6 g Poly, 10.4 g Sat); 64 mg Cholesterol; 17 g Carbohydrate; 1 g Fibre; 14 g Protein; 399 mg Sodium

Pictured on page 43.

BAKED SPECKLED SPIRALS: Arrange slices, cut-side down, on greased baking sheet. Lightly brush top of each with cooking oil. Bake in 350°F (175°C) oven for 10 to 12 minutes until edges are golden.

Kids Can Help

Grating cheese. Stirring filling. Rolling up tortillas.

Top: Creamy Chicken Wrap, page 44
Bottom: Speckled Spirals, above

Creamy Chicken Wrap

Try a variety of cream cheese flavours for a new taste sensation every time!
Serve with Iced Apple Tea, page 12.

CHICKEN SALAD FILLING

Spreadable cream cheese (your favourite)	3 tbsp.	50 mL
Salad dressing (or mayonnaise)	1 tbsp.	15 mL
Prepared mustard	1 tsp.	5 mL
Salt, just a pinch		
Finely chopped cooked chicken	1/3 cup	75 mL
Grated carrot	3 tbsp.	50 mL
Finely chopped celery	3 tbsp.	50 mL
Finely chopped green onion	1 – 2 tbsp.	15 – 30 mL
Whole wheat flour tortilla (9 inch, 22 cm, diameter)	1	1

Chicken Salad Filling: Combine first 4 ingredients in medium bowl.

Add next 4 ingredients. Stir well. Makes about 1 cup (250 mL) filling.

Spoon filling across centre of tortilla, almost to edge. Fold sides over filling. Roll up from bottom to enclose filling. To serve, cut in half diagonally. Makes 1 wrap.

1 wrap: 418 Calories; 27.6 g Total Fat (9.9 g Mono, 4.4 g Poly, 11.4 g Sat); 97 mg Cholesterol; 22 g Carbohydrate; 3 g Fibre; 22 g Protein; 524 mg Sodium

Pictured on page 43.

Kids Can Help

Peeling and grating carrot. Stirring filling. Rolling up tortilla.

Turkey And Cuke Sandwich

Cranberry sauce adds sweetness and cucumbers add crunch to this hearty sandwich.
To take to school, pack cucumber separately and add just before eating.

Process cheese spread	1 tbsp.	15 mL
Whole grain (or your favourite) bread slices	2	2
Cranberry sauce	1 tbsp.	15 mL

(continued on next page)

| Thin English cucumber slices (with peel) | 6 | 6 |
| Deli turkey breast (about 2 slices) | 2 oz. | 57 g |

Spread cheese spread evenly on 1 side of 1 bread slice. Spread cranberry sauce evenly on 1 side of second bread slice.

Layer cucumber and turkey slices on top of cheese spread. Cover with second bread slice, cranberry-side down. To serve, cut in half or into quarters. Makes 1 sandwich.

1 sandwich: 296 Calories; 9.1 g Total Fat (2.6 g Mono, 1.6 g Poly, 3.7 g Sat); 39 mg Cholesterol; 36 g Carbohydrate; 4 g Fibre; 21 g Protein; 953 mg Sodium

Pictured above.

Variation: Omit deli turkey breast slices. Use same amount of leftover roast turkey.

Kids Can Help

Spreading and layering ingredients.

Donair Buns

Well-seasoned pork and beef rolls topped with a cool, creamy dill sauce and fresh vegetables. The whole family will be asking for more! Cool completely before packing for school.

DONAIR ROLL

Lean ground pork	1/2 lb.	225 g
Lean ground beef	1/2 lb.	225 g
Fine dry bread crumbs	1/4 cup	60 mL
Parsley flakes	2 tsp.	10 mL
Garlic clove, minced (or 1/4 tsp., 1 mL, powder), optional	1	1
Chili powder	1 tsp.	5 mL
Salt	1 tsp.	5 mL
Ground cumin	1/2 tsp.	2 mL
Cayenne pepper	1/16 tsp.	0.5 mL

DONAIR SAUCE

Low-fat plain yogurt	1/2 cup	125 mL
Light mayonnaise (not salad dressing)	1/3 cup	75 mL
Lemon juice	1 tsp.	5 mL
Dill weed	1/2 tsp.	2 mL
Hamburger (or hot dog) buns, split	8	8
Finely chopped red onion	1/3 cup	75 mL
Chopped or torn lettuce (your favourite), lightly packed	1 cup	250 mL
Chopped tomato	1 1/2 cups	375 mL

Donair Roll: Process first 9 ingredients in food processor for about 1 minute until pork and beef are finely ground. Turn out onto work surface. Shape mixture into 11 inch (28 cm) long roll. Place on greased wire rack set in baking sheet with sides. Cover top of roll with foil, leaving bottom uncovered. Bake in 275°F (140°C) oven for about 3 hours until firm and no longer pink inside. Remove from oven. Wrap roll in foil. Let stand for 15 minutes. Discard foil. Cut roll diagonally into 1/4 inch (6 mm) slices, for a total of about 36 slices.

Donair Sauce: Combine first 4 ingredients in small bowl. Makes about 1 cup (250 mL) sauce.

(continued on next page)

Divide and spread sauce on top and bottom half of each bun. Divide and layer onion, donair roll slices, lettuce and chopped tomato on bottom half of each bun. Cover with top halves of buns. Makes 8 donair buns.

1 donair bun: *304 Calories; 14 g Total Fat (6.7 g Mono, 2 g Poly, 4 g Sat); 34 mg Cholesterol; 28 g Carbohydrate; 2 g Fibre; 16 g Protein; 688 mg Sodium*

Pictured below.

Kids Can Help

Stirring sauce. Layering ingredients.

Cheese-Wrapped Dogs

Kids will enjoy the crunchy cornmeal pastry that makes these hot dogs extra special. Make ahead and freeze.

All–purpose flour	1 1/4 cups	300 mL
Yellow cornmeal	1/4 cup	60 mL
Baking powder	1 tbsp.	15 mL
Cold hard margarine (or butter), cut up	1/3 cup	75 mL
Milk	1/2 cup	125 mL
Wieners (your favourite)	6	6
Grated medium (or mild) Cheddar cheese	3/4 cup	175 mL

Combine first 3 ingredients in medium bowl. Cut in margarine until mixture resembles coarse crumbs. Make a well in centre.

Add milk to well. Stir until just moistened. Turn out dough onto lightly floured surface. Knead 5 or 6 times. Roll out or press into 12 inch (30 cm) square. Cut in half. Cut each half into 3 equal portions, for a total of 6.

Place 1 wiener lengthwise down centre of 1 dough portion. Sprinkle 2 tbsp. (30 mL) cheese evenly over top. Fold both long sides over wiener. Pinch together to seal. Repeat with remaining dough portions, wieners and cheese, for a total of 6 rolls. Arrange rolls, seam-side down, evenly spaced apart on greased baking sheet. Bake in 425°F (220°C) oven for 12 to 15 minutes until golden. Makes 6 hot dogs.

1 hot dog: 398 Calories; 25 g Total Fat (12.6 g Mono, 2.2 g Poly, 8.8 g Sat); 35 mg Cholesterol; 30 g Carbohydrate; 1 g Fibre; 13 g Protein; 789 mg Sodium

Pictured on page 49.

Kids Can Help

Cutting margarine into dry ingredients. Grating and sprinkling cheese.

Top: Round-Up Wrap, page 50
Bottom: Cheese-Wrapped Dogs, above

Round-Up Wrap

Save leftovers from a roast chicken dinner. Round them up the next day to make this tasty tortilla wrap. Good hot or cold.

Leftover mashed potatoes	1/3 cup	75 mL
Chopped cooked chicken	1/2 cup	125 mL
Whole wheat flour tortilla (9 inch, 22 cm, diameter)	1	1
Sour cream	2 tbsp.	30 mL
Barbecue sauce	3 tbsp.	50 mL
Leftover kernel corn	3 tbsp.	50 mL

Reheat mashed potatoes and chicken. Cover chicken to keep warm. Spread potatoes evenly in centre of tortilla, leaving 2 1/2 inch (6.4 cm) border around edge.

Spread sour cream on potatoes. Spread barbecue sauce on sour cream. Scatter chicken and corn over sauce. Fold sides over filling. Roll up from bottom to enclose filling. To serve, cut in half diagonally. Makes 1 wrap.

1 wrap: 583 Calories; 16.3 g Total Fat (4.8 g Mono, 3 g Poly, 6.7 g Sat); 87 mg Cholesterol; 80 g Carbohydrate; 11 g Fibre; 35 g Protein; 1194 mg Sodium

Pictured on page 49.

Variation: Omit chicken. Use same amount of leftover roast beef or steak.

Kids Can Help

Spreading ingredients. Scattering chicken and corn.

Grilled Pasta Sandwich

*Kids will love this messy but fun-to-eat sandwich.
Grill in a frying pan if you don't have a sandwich maker or 2-sided grill.*

Hard margarine (or butter), softened	2 tsp.	10 mL
Thick slices of whole grain (or your favourite) bread	2	2
Grated medium (or mild) Cheddar cheese	1/4 cup	60 mL
Canned pasta in tomato sauce	1/4 cup	60 mL

(continued on next page)

Spread 1 tsp. (5 mL) margarine on 1 side of each bread slice. Place 1 bread slice, margarine-side down, on cutting board.

Sprinkle with cheese. Spoon pasta onto cheese. Cover with second bread slice, margarine side-up. Place in hot sandwich maker or 2-sided grill. Close lid. Cook for 3 to 4 minutes until bread is golden and cheese is melted. To serve, cut in half or into quarters. Makes 1 sandwich.

1 sandwich: 450 Calories; 21.7 g Total Fat (9.4 g Mono, 2 g Poly, 8.8 g Sat); 34 mg Cholesterol; 50 g Carbohydrate; 8 g Fibre; 17 g Protein; 980 mg Sodium

Pictured below.

Kids Can Help

Grating and sprinkling cheese. Opening can.

Chip Chicken In A Wrap

Potato chips make an especially good coating for tender chicken strips nestled in tasty tortillas! To pack for school, omit lettuce.

HONEY MUSTARD SAUCE

Salad dressing (or mayonnaise)	1/2 cup	125 mL
Liquid honey	2 tbsp.	30 mL
Prepared mustard	2 tsp.	10 mL
Large egg	1	1
Milk	1 tbsp.	15 mL
Finely crushed potato chips (your favourite)	1 cup	250 mL
Yellow cornmeal	1/4 cup	60 mL
Boneless, skinless chicken breast halves	1 lb.	454 g
Flour tortillas (9 inch, 22 cm, diameter)	4	4
Green leaf lettuce leaves (optional)	8	8

Honey Mustard Sauce: Combine first 3 ingredients in small bowl. Makes about 2/3 cup (150 mL) sauce. Set aside.

Beat egg and milk with fork in medium bowl.

Combine crushed potato chips and cornmeal in shallow medium dish.

Cut each chicken breast half diagonally into 4 or 5 strips. Dip each strip into egg mixture. Press both sides of each strip into potato chip mixture until coated. Arrange chicken strips evenly spaced apart on greased baking sheet with sides. Bake in 400°F (205°C) oven for 15 to 20 minutes until chicken is no longer pink inside.

Spread about 2 1/2 tbsp. (37 mL) sauce evenly on 1 tortilla, almost to edge. Place 2 lettuce leaves on top of sauce. Arrange 3 to 4 chicken strips on top of lettuce across centre of tortilla. Fold sides over filling. Roll up from bottom to enclose filling. Repeat with remaining ingredients, for a total of 4 wraps. To serve, cut each wrap in half diagonally. Makes 4 wraps.

1 wrap: 626 Calories; 28.1 g Total Fat (14.1 g Mono, 8.8 g Poly, 3.3 g Sat); 123 mg Cholesterol; 60 g Carbohydrate; 2 g Fibre; 32 g Protein; 589 mg Sodium

Pictured on page 53.

Kids Can Help

Beating egg and milk. Stirring and spreading sauce.
Layering ingredients. Rolling up tortillas.

Top: Bacon And Egg Wrap, page 54
Bottom: Chip Chicken In A Wrap, above

Bacon And Egg Wrap

Sweet, smoky barbecue sauce adds zip to this wrap full of breakfast fixings!
Serve with Very Berry, page 14.

Large eggs	2	2
Grated medium (or mild) Cheddar cheese	2 tbsp.	30 mL
Milk	1 tbsp.	15 mL
Finely sliced green onion (or chives), optional	1 tbsp.	15 mL
Cooking oil	1 tsp.	5 mL
Barbecue sauce	1 tbsp.	15 mL
Flour tortilla (9 inch, 22 cm, diameter)	1	1
Bacon slices, cooked crisp and crumbled	3	3
Thin tomato slices	3	3

Beat first 4 ingredients with fork in small bowl.

Heat cooking oil in small frying pan on medium. Pour egg mixture into pan. Reduce heat to medium-low. Stir slowly and constantly with spatula, scraping side and bottom of pan until egg is set and liquid is evaporated. Remove from heat.

Spread barbecue sauce evenly on tortilla, almost to edge. Spoon egg mixture evenly onto barbecue sauce.

Scatter bacon over egg mixture. Arrange tomato slices on bacon. Fold sides over filling. Roll up from bottom to enclose filling. To serve, cut in half diagonally. Makes 1 wrap.

1 wrap: 556 Calories; 33.1 g Total Fat (14.1 g Mono, 5.6 g Poly, 10.5 g Sat); 463 mg Cholesterol; 36 g Carbohydrate; 3 g Fibre; 28 g Protein; 910 mg Sodium

Pictured on page 53.

Kids Can Help

Breaking eggs. Grating cheese. Spreading barbecue sauce. Crumbling bacon.

Tuna Quesadilla

A great way to use canned tuna—not just for sandwiches anymore!

TUNA FILLING

Canned flaked tuna, drained	1/4 cup	60 mL
Grated medium (or mild) Cheddar cheese	3 tbsp.	50 mL
Mild (or medium) salsa	2 tbsp.	30 mL
Finely chopped green onion	1 tbsp.	15 mL
Whole wheat flour tortilla (9 inch, 22 cm, diameter)	1	1

Tuna Filling: Combine first 4 ingredients in small bowl. Makes about 2/3 cup (150 mL) filling.

Spread filling evenly on 1/2 of tortilla, almost to edge. Fold other 1/2 of tortilla over filling. Spray large frying pan with cooking spray. Heat on medium-low until hot. Cook quesadilla for 2 to 3 minutes per side until golden and cheese is melted. To serve, cut into 4 wedges. Makes 1 quesadilla.

1 quesadilla: 404 Calories; 10.9 g Total Fat (2.7 g Mono, 1.7 g Poly, 5.3 g Sat); 40 mg Cholesterol; 55 g Carbohydrate; 8 g Fibre; 25 g Protein; 885 mg Sodium

Pictured above.

Kids Can Help

Grating cheese. Washing green onion. Spreading filling. Folding tortilla.

Pizza Burgers

Something a bit different that's sure to become a favourite. Chicken patties may be frozen—just add toppings and heat in microwave for a quick lunch.

Large egg	1	1
Finely diced deli pepperoni sticks	1/2 cup	125 mL
Fine dry bread crumbs	1/3 cup	75 mL
Chopped green onion	2 tbsp.	30 mL
Seasoned salt	1 tsp.	5 mL
Dried whole oregano	3/4 tsp.	4 mL
Pepper	1/8 tsp.	0.5 mL
Lean ground chicken	1 lb.	454 g
Pizza sauce	6 tbsp.	100 mL
Process part-skim mozzarella cheese slices	6	6
Hamburger buns, split and toasted (buttered, optional)	6	6

Beat egg with fork in large bowl. Add next 6 ingredients. Stir well.

Add ground chicken. Mix well. Divide into 6 equal portions. Shape each portion into 4 inch (10 cm) diameter patty. Arrange patties evenly spaced apart on greased broiler pan. Broil 6 inches (15 cm) from heat in oven for about 8 minutes per side until no longer pink inside.

Spread 1 tbsp. (15 mL) pizza sauce on each patty. Top each with 1 cheese slice. Broil for about 2 minutes until cheese is melted. Place 1 patty on bottom half of each bun. Cover with top halves of buns. Makes 6 pizza burgers.

1 pizza burger: 391 Calories; 14 g Total Fat (5.2 g Mono, 1.9 g Poly, 3.6 g Sat); 99 mg Cholesterol; 33 g Carbohydrate; 2 g Fibre; 32 g Protein; 1377 mg Sodium

Pictured on page 57.

Kids Can Help

Beating egg. Measuring dry ingredients. Unwrapping cheese slices. Toasting buns.

Pizza Burgers, above

Lasagne Spirals

Cheesy spinach filling rolled in tender lasagna noodles and smothered in your favourite pasta sauce. The whole family will love these.

Lasagna noodles	12	12
Boiling water	12 cups	3 L
Salt (optional)	1 1/2 tsp.	7 mL
Large eggs	2	2
Chopped fresh spinach, stems removed, lightly packed	2 1/4 cups	550 mL
Ricotta cheese	2 cups	500 mL
Grated part-skim mozzarella cheese	3/4 cup	175 mL
Grated Parmesan cheese	1/3 cup	75 mL
Chopped fresh basil (or 1 1/2 tsp., 7 mL, dried)	2 tbsp.	30 mL
Pasta sauce	4 cups	1 L
Grated part-skim mozzarella cheese	1 cup	250 mL

Cook lasagna noodles in boiling water and salt in large uncovered pot or Dutch oven for 14 to 16 minutes, stirring occasionally, until tender but firm. Drain.

Beat eggs with fork in large bowl. Add next 5 ingredients. Stir well. Makes about 3 1/2 cups (875 mL) filling. Spread 1/3 cup (75 mL) filling on 1 lasagna noodle. Roll up, jelly roll-style, from short end. Repeat with remaining filling and noodles.

Spread 1 cup (250 mL) pasta sauce evenly in greased 9 × 13 inch (22 × 33 cm) pan. Arrange spirals, seam-side down, in single layer on top of sauce. Spoon remaining pasta sauce onto spirals. Cover with foil. Bake in 350°F (175°C) oven for about 40 minutes until heated through. Discard foil.

Sprinkle second amount of mozzarella cheese over top. Bake, uncovered, for about 15 minutes until cheese is melted. Freezes well. Makes 12 spirals.

1 spiral: 316 Calories; 14.5 g Total Fat (5.1 g Mono, 1.7 g Poly, 6.8 g Sat); 70 mg Cholesterol; 31 g Carbohydrate; 2 g Fibre; 16 g Protein; 629 mg Sodium

Pictured on page 59.

Kids Can Help

Stirring spinach filling. Spreading filling on noodles and rolling them up. Spreading sauce in pan. Spooning sauce over spirals in pan. Grating cheese.

Top: Mushroom Pasta, page 60
Bottom: Lasagne Spirals, above

Mushroom Pasta

*Earthy mushrooms and smoky bacon are a delicious pairing
in a creamy, cheesy sauce. Serve with a salad.*

Medium bow (or other) pasta (about 6 oz., 170 g)	2 cups	500 mL
Boiling water	9 cups	2.25 L
Salt	1 tsp.	5 mL
Cooking oil	2 tsp.	10 mL
Sliced fresh white mushrooms	2 cups	500 mL
Chopped onion	1/2 cup	125 mL
All-purpose flour	1 tbsp.	15 mL
Half-and-half cream (or homogenized milk)	1 cup	250 mL
Bacon slices, cooked crisp and crumbled	3	3
Grated medium (or mild) Cheddar cheese	1/3 cup	75 mL
Chopped fresh parsley (or 1 1/2 tsp., 7 mL, flakes)	2 tbsp.	30 mL

Cook pasta in boiling water and salt in large uncovered pot or Dutch oven for 14 to 16 minutes, stirring occasionally, until tender but firm. Drain. Return pasta to same pot. Cover to keep warm.

Heat cooking oil in large frying pan on medium. Add mushrooms and onion. Cook for 5 to 10 minutes, stirring often, until onion is softened.

Sprinkle with flour. Heat and stir for 1 minute. Add cream and bacon. Reduce heat to medium-low. Heat and stir until boiling and thickened. Add to pasta. Toss until coated.

Add cheese and parsley. Toss. Makes 3 cups (750 mL).

1 cup (250 mL): 461 Calories; 20.3 g Total Fat (7.1 g Mono, 2.2 g Poly, 9.6 g Sat); 46 mg Cholesterol; 53 g Carbohydrate; 3 g Fibre; 17 g Protein; 226 mg Sodium

Pictured on page 59.

Kids Can Help

Measuring dry ingredients. Slicing mushrooms. Grating cheese.

Dressed-Up Pasta

Dress up lunch with bow ties! Salsa and cheese make a zesty sauce.

Medium bow (or other) pasta (about 3 oz., 85 g)	1 cup	250 mL
Boiling water	5 cups	1.25 L
Salt	1 tsp.	5 mL
Bacon slices, cooked crisp and crumbled	4	4
Mild salsa	1 cup	250 mL
Process cheese spread	1/4 cup	60 mL
Hard margarine (or butter)	2 tsp.	10 mL
Grated medium (or mild) Cheddar cheese	1/2 cup	125 mL

Cook pasta in boiling water and salt in large uncovered saucepan for 14 to 16 minutes, stirring occasionally, until tender but firm. Drain. Return pasta to same pan.

Add next 4 ingredients. Heat and stir on low for 1 to 2 minutes until cheese spread is melted. Remove to serving dish.

Sprinkle with Cheddar cheese. Makes 2 cups (500 mL).

1 cup (250 mL): 516 Calories; 27.9 g Total Fat (10.5 g Mono, 2.1 g Poly, 13.8 g Sat); 60 mg Cholesterol; 43 g Carbohydrate; 4 g Fibre; 24 g Protein; 1312 mg Sodium

Pictured above.

Kids Can Help

Measuring pasta. Grating and sprinkling Cheddar cheese.

Tortellini And Tomato Sauce

Bundles of pasta smothered in a tangy, chunky tomato sauce everyone will enjoy.

Package of fresh cheese-filled tortellini (or your favourite)	12 oz.	350 g
Boiling water	6 cups	1.5 L
Salt	1/4 tsp.	1 mL
Cooking oil	2 tsp.	10 mL
Finely chopped onion	1/2 cup	125 mL
Garlic clove, minced (or 1/4 tsp., 1 mL, powder), optional	1	1
Can of diced tomatoes (with juice)	14 oz.	398 mL
Balsamic vinegar	1 tsp.	5 mL
Granulated sugar	1/2 tsp.	2 mL
Salt, just a pinch		
Grated Parmesan cheese	1 tbsp.	15 mL

Cook tortellini in boiling water and first amount of salt in large uncovered pot or Dutch oven for about 5 minutes, stirring occasionally, until tender but firm. Drain. Return tortellini to same pot. Cover to keep warm.

Heat cooking oil in medium frying pan on medium. Add onion. Cook for 5 to 10 minutes, stirring often, until softened.

Add garlic. Heat and stir for 1 to 2 minutes until fragrant.

Add next 4 ingredients. Stir. Bring to a boil. Reduce heat to medium-low. Simmer, uncovered, for about 5 minutes, stirring occasionally, until slightly thickened. Add to tortellini. Toss gently. Remove to serving dish.

Sprinkle with Parmesan cheese. Makes about 3 cups (750 mL).

1 cup (250 mL): 321 Calories; 14 g Total Fat (2.1 g Mono, 1.1 g Poly, 0.7 g Sat); 72 mg Cholesterol; 34 g Carbohydrate; 2 g Fibre; 16 g Protein; 556 mg Sodium

Pictured on front cover.

Kids Can Help

Measuring dry ingredients. Sprinkling Parmesan cheese.

Ham And Broccoli Pasta

Tender noodles with ham, broccoli and tomato. This makes just enough
for two children, or one hungry teenager! A great way to use leftovers.

Penne (or other tube) pasta (about 1 1/2 oz., 43 g)	1/2 cup	125 mL
Boiling water	4 cups	1 L
Salt	1/2 tsp.	2 mL
Hard margarine (or butter)	1 tsp.	5 mL
Cooking oil	1 tsp.	5 mL
Diced cooked ham	1/2 cup	125 mL
Medium tomato, chopped	1	1
Frozen broccoli, thawed and chopped	1/2 cup	125 mL
Milk	2 – 4 tbsp.	30 – 60 mL
Grated Parmesan cheese	2 tbsp.	30 mL
Chopped green onion	1 tbsp.	15 mL

Cook pasta in boiling water and salt in uncovered medium saucepan for 12 to 15 minutes, stirring occasionally, until tender but firm. Drain. Return pasta to same pan.

Add margarine. Stir until melted. Cover to keep warm.

Heat cooking oil in medium frying pan on medium. Add ham. Heat and stir for 1 to 2 minutes until starting to brown.

Add next 4 ingredients. Stir. Cover. Cook for about 2 minutes, stirring occasionally, until broccoli is tender-crisp.

Add green onion. Stir. Add to pasta. Toss well. Makes 2 1/4 cups (550 mL).

1 cup (250 mL): 219 Calories; 9.1 g Total Fat (4.4 g Mono, 1.5 g Poly, 2.8 g Sat); 24 mg Cholesterol; 20 g Carbohydrate; 2 g Fibre; 15 g Protein; 642 mg Sodium

Pictured on page 65.

Kids Can Help

Measuring dry ingredients. Washing vegetables. Grating Parmesan cheese.

Macaroni Tuna Bake

Salsa and cheese topping adds zip to this delicious lunch.
Add a tossed salad, cucumber slices or carrot sticks for a balanced meal.

Elbow macaroni (about 6 oz., 170 g)	1 1/2 cups	375 mL
Boiling water	8 cups	2 L
Salt	1 tsp.	5 mL
Hard margarine (or butter)	3 tbsp.	50 mL
Finely chopped onion	2/3 cup	150 mL
Finely chopped celery	1/3 cup	75 mL
All-purpose flour	3 tbsp.	50 mL
Milk	2 cups	500 mL
Large eggs	6	6
Dijon mustard	1 tbsp.	15 mL
Parsley flakes	1 tsp.	5 mL
Salt	1/2 tsp.	2 mL
Pepper	1/4 tsp.	1 mL
Cans of white tuna packed in water (4 1/4 oz., 120 g, each), drained and flaked	2	2
Mild (or medium) salsa	1 cup	250 mL
Grated medium Cheddar cheese	1 cup	250 mL

Cook macaroni in boiling water and first amount of salt in large uncovered pot or Dutch oven for 10 to 12 minutes, stirring occasionally, until tender but firm. Drain. Return macaroni to same pot. Cover to keep warm.

Melt margarine in medium saucepan on medium. Add onion and celery. Cook for 5 to 10 minutes, stirring often, until onion is softened.

Add flour. Heat and stir for 1 minute. Slowly add milk, stirring constantly. Heat and stir for about 5 minutes until boiling and thickened. Remove from heat.

Beat next 5 ingredients with whisk in large bowl. Add hot milk mixture. Beat until smooth. Add to macaroni. Stir.

Add tuna. Stir well. Spread evenly in greased 3 quart (3 L) shallow baking dish. Bake, uncovered, in 350°F (175°C) oven for 20 minutes. Stir. Bake for 10 minutes. Stir.

(continued on next page)

Spread salsa on top. Sprinkle with cheese. Bake for about 10 minutes until cheese is melted. Let stand for 10 minutes. Freezes well. Makes 7 cups (1.75 L).

1 cup (250 mL): 353 Calories; 17 g Total Fat (6.9 g Mono, 1.8 g Poly, 6.7 g Sat); 214 mg Cholesterol; 28 g Carbohydrate; 2 g Fibre; 21 g Protein; 640 mg Sodium

Pictured below.

Kids Can Help

Measuring macaroni. Stirring macaroni and sauce. Adding tuna. Grating cheese.

Top: Ham And Broccoli Pasta, page 63
Bottom: Macaroni Tuna Bake, page 64

Stuffed Pasta Shells

For kids of all ages. Just as tasty hot or cold. Freezes well.

Jumbo shell pasta	16	16
Boiling water	12 cups	3 L
Salt	1 1/2 tsp.	7 mL
Hard margarine (or butter)	2 tbsp.	30 mL
Chopped onion	1/2 cup	125 mL
Garlic clove, minced (or 1/4 tsp., 1 mL, powder), optional	1	1
Water	1 tbsp.	15 mL
Box of frozen chopped spinach, thawed and squeezed dry	10 oz.	300 g
Ricotta cheese	1 cup	250 mL
Grated Parmesan cheese	1/3 cup	75 mL
Large egg, fork-beaten	1	1
Salt	1/4 tsp.	1 mL
Ground nutmeg	1/8 tsp.	0.5 mL
Grated part-skim mozzarella cheese	1/2 cup	125 mL

Cook pasta in boiling water and first amount of salt in large uncovered pot or Dutch oven for 13 to 15 minutes, stirring occasionally, until tender but firm. Drain. Rinse with cold water. Drain well. Return pasta to same pot. Set aside.

Melt margarine in small frying pan on medium. Add onion. Cook for 5 to 10 minutes, stirring often, until softened.

Add garlic. Heat and stir for 1 to 2 minutes until fragrant. Cool.

Drizzle water in ungreased 3 quart (3 L) shallow baking dish.

Combine next 6 ingredients in medium bowl. Add onion mixture. Stir well. Makes about 2 cups (500 mL) filling. Spoon 2 tbsp. (30 mL) filling into each pasta shell. Arrange stuffed pasta shells in single layer in prepared baking dish.

Sprinkle mozzarella cheese over top of shells. Cover with foil. Bake in 350°F (175°C) oven for about 20 minutes until heated through and cheese is melted. Discard foil. Let stand for 5 minutes. Makes 16 stuffed pasta shells.

1 stuffed pasta shell: 97 Calories; 5.3 g Total Fat (2 g Mono, 0.4 g Poly, 2.6 g Sat); 26 mg Cholesterol; 7 g Carbohydrate; 1 g Fibre; 6 g Protein; 143 mg Sodium

Pictured on page 67.

(continued on next page)

Squeezing water from spinach. Stuffing pasta shells.
Grating and sprinkling mozzarella cheese.

Veggie Noodle Stir-Fry

An attractive dish, full of colour and texture. Mild spices and full of flavour.

Medium (spiral) egg noodles	8 oz.	225 g
Boiling water	12 cups	3 L
Salt	1 1/2 tsp.	7 mL
Sesame oil, for flavour	1 tsp.	5 mL
Water	1 cup	250 mL
Cornstarch	2 tsp.	10 mL
Soy sauce	1 tbsp.	15 mL
Chicken (or vegetable) bouillon powder	1 tsp.	5 mL
Cooking oil	1 tbsp.	15 mL
Finely chopped cabbage	1 1/2 cups	375 mL
Medium onion, thinly sliced	1	1
Medium carrot, grated	1	1
Red (or green) medium pepper, seeds and ribs removed, thinly sliced	1	1
Sliced fresh white mushrooms	1 cup	250 mL
Snow peas, trimmed	6 oz.	170 g
Salt	1 tsp.	5 mL
Pepper	1/8 tsp.	0.5 mL

Cook noodles in boiling water and first amount of salt in large uncovered pot or Dutch oven for 5 to 7 minutes, stirring occasionally, until tender but firm. Drain. Return noodles to same pot.

Add sesame oil. Stir until noodles are coated. Cover to keep warm.

Stir water into cornstarch in small bowl until smooth. Add soy sauce and bouillon powder. Stir. Set aside.

Heat wok or large frying pan on medium-high until very hot. Add cooking oil. Add cabbage, onion and carrot. Stir-fry for about 3 minutes until vegetables are slightly softened.

Add remaining 5 ingredients. Stir-fry for about 2 minutes until red pepper and snow peas are tender-crisp. Stir cornstarch mixture. Slowly add to vegetable mixture, stirring constantly, until boiling and thickened. Add noodles. Heat and stir for 1 to 2 minutes until heated through. Makes about 8 cups (2 L).

1 cup (250 mL): 163 Calories; 3.8 g Total Fat (1.6 g Mono, 1.2 g Poly, 0.5 g Sat); 27 mg Cholesterol; 27 g Carbohydrate; 2 g Fibre; 6 g Protein; 523 mg Sodium

Pictured on page 69.

(continued on next page)

Washing vegetables. Grating carrot. Removing seeds and ribs from red pepper. Trimming snow peas.

Pork Bites

Make these ahead and freeze so you have a quick answer when the kids ask, "What's for lunch?" Flaky puff pastry makes these especially good. Serve with mustard for dipping.

Large egg	1	1
Finely chopped onion	1/3 cup	75 mL
Fine dry bread crumbs	1/3 cup	75 mL
Ketchup	4 tsp.	20 mL
Salt	1/8 tsp.	0.5 mL
Pepper	1/16 tsp.	0.5 mL
Lean ground pork	3/4 lb.	340 g
Package of frozen puff pastry, thawed according to package directions	14 oz.	397 g
Large egg, fork-beaten	1	1

Beat first egg with fork in large bowl. Add next 5 ingredients. Stir well.

Add ground pork. Mix well. Divide into 4 equal portions. Shape each portion into 10 1/2 inch (26 cm) long roll. Place rolls on plastic wrap-lined baking sheet. Freeze, uncovered, for about 2 hours until firm.

Roll out 1/2 of puff pastry (1 square) on lightly floured surface to 10 inch (25 cm) square. Keep remaining pastry chilled. Cut pastry square into 2 equal rectangles. Place 1 pork roll at edge of long side of 1 rectangle. Keep remaining rectangle covered to prevent drying. Brush opposite edge of long side with second amount of egg. Roll up. Press seam against roll to seal. Place, seam-side down, on cutting board. Brush roll with egg. Cut into 1 inch (2.5 cm) slices. Arrange slices evenly spaced apart on 1/2 of greased baking sheet. Repeat with second rectangle and 1 pork roll, arranging slices on other 1/2 of same baking sheet. Bake in 400°F (205°C) oven for about 20 minutes until golden. Repeat with remaining pastry square and 2 pork rolls. Freezes well. Makes 40 pork bites.

1 pork bite: 81 Calories; 5.3 g Total Fat (1.5 g Mono, 2.3 g Poly, 1.1 g Sat); 16 mg Cholesterol; 5 g Carbohydrate; trace Fibre; 3 g Protein; 54 mg Sodium

Pictured on page 71.

(continued on next page)

Kids Can Help

Beating eggs. Rolling pastry. Brushing pastry with egg.

Top: Pork Bites, page 70
Bottom: Broccoli Cups, page 72

Broccoli Cups

Savoury bacon and broccoli tarts with a pleasant, quiche-like texture.
These will quickly disappear! Double the recipe and freeze for a quick lunch.

BROCCOLI FILLING

Cooking oil	2 tsp.	10 mL
Chopped broccoli	1 cup	250 mL
Chopped fresh white mushrooms	1 cup	250 mL
Sliced green onion	1/4 cup	60 mL
Large eggs	2	2
Sour cream	1/4 cup	60 mL
Grated medium (or mild) Cheddar cheese	1/4 cup	60 mL
Bacon slices, cooked crisp and crumbled	4	4
Pepper, sprinkle		
Frozen tart shells, thawed	12	12

Broccoli Filling: Heat cooking oil in medium frying pan on medium. Add next 3 ingredients. Cook for 5 to 10 minutes, stirring occasionally, until mushrooms start to brown. Cool slightly.

Beat next 3 ingredients with whisk in medium bowl.

Add bacon, pepper and broccoli mixture. Stir well. Makes 1 1/2 cups (375 mL) filling.

Arrange tart shells on ungreased baking sheet. Spoon 2 tbsp. (30 mL) filling into each shell. Spread evenly. Bake on bottom rack in 350°F (175°C) oven for 30 to 35 minutes until pastry is golden and filling is set. Makes 12 broccoli cups.

1 broccoli cup: 118 Calories; 8.3 g Total Fat (3.7 g Mono, 1 g Poly, 3 g Sat); 42 mg Cholesterol;
7 g Carbohydrate; trace Fibre; 3 g Protein; 145 mg Sodium

Pictured on page 71.

Kids Can Help

Grating cheese. Stirring egg mixture. Crumbling bacon.
Arranging tart shells on baking sheet. Filling tart shells.

Sunnyside Pizza

A pizza that tastes like breakfast. The egg in the centre will really crack up the kids!

Prebaked pizza crust (6 inch, 15 cm, diameter)	1	1
Mild (or medium) salsa	3 tbsp.	50 mL
Grated medium (or mild) Cheddar cheese	2 tbsp.	30 mL
Bacon slices, cooked almost crisp and diced	3	3
Tomato slices	3	3
Large egg	1	1
Grated medium (or mild) Cheddar cheese	3 tbsp.	50 mL

Place pizza crust on ungreased baking sheet. Spread salsa evenly on crust, almost to edge. Sprinkle first amount of cheese over salsa, leaving 2 to 3 inch (5 to 7.5 cm) circle in centre unsprinkled.

Scatter bacon over cheese. Arrange tomato slices over bacon.

Break egg into circle. Sprinkle second amount of cheese over egg. Bake in 450°F (230°C) oven for about 15 minutes until crust is crisp and egg is set. Cuts into 4 wedges.

1 wedge: 132 Calories; 7.2 g Total Fat (2.5 g Mono, 0.6 g Poly, 3.1 g Sat); 67 mg Cholesterol; 10 g Carbohydrate; trace Fibre; 7 g Protein; 266 mg Sodium

Pictured on page 75.

Kids Can Help

Spreading salsa. Grating cheese. Breaking egg into circle.

Hawaiian Chicken Pizza

A new twist on an old favourite.

Prebaked pizza crust (6 inch, 15 cm, diameter)	1	1
Pizza sauce	3 tbsp.	50 mL
Grated Cheddar (or part-skim mozzarella) cheese	2 tbsp.	30 mL
Sliced green pepper	1/4 cup	60 mL
Pineapple tidbits, well drained	1/4 cup	60 mL
Chopped cooked chicken	1/3 cup	75 mL
Chopped green onion	2 tbsp.	30 mL
Grated Cheddar (or part-skim mozzarella) cheese	1/4 cup	60 mL

Place pizza crust on ungreased baking sheet. Spread pizza sauce evenly on crust, almost to edge. Sprinkle first amount of cheese over sauce.

Scatter next 5 ingredients, in order given, over cheese. Bake in 450°F (230°C) oven for 10 to 15 minutes until crust is crisp and cheese is melted. Cuts into 4 wedges.

1 wedge: 134 Calories; 5.8 g Total Fat (1.7 g Mono, 0.5 g Poly, 2.7 g Sat); 23 mg Cholesterol; 12 g Carbohydrate; 1 g Fibre; 8 g Protein; 225 mg Sodium

Pictured on page 75.

Kids Can Help

Spreading pizza sauce. Grating cheese. Washing vegetables.
Scattering toppings on pizza.

Tip: To slice meat easily, place in freezer for about 30 minutes until just starting to freeze. If using from frozen state, partially thaw before cutting.

Top: Sunnyside Pizza, page 73
Bottom: Hawaiian Chicken Pizza, above

Ham Tomato Pizza

Tastes like a ham and tomato sandwich—only better! Colourful and inviting.

Prebaked pizza crust (12 inch, 30 cm, diameter)	1	1
Grated medium (or mild) Cheddar cheese	1/2 cup	125 mL
Diced cooked ham	1 cup	250 mL
Finely chopped celery	2/3 cup	150 mL
Sliced green onion	1/4 cup	60 mL
Salad dressing (or mayonnaise)	1/4 cup	60 mL
Seasoned salt	1/4 tsp.	1 mL
Medium tomatoes, thinly sliced	2	2
Grated medium (or mild) Cheddar cheese	3/4 cup	175 mL
Salad dressing (or mayonnaise)	1/3 cup	75 mL

Place pizza crust on ungreased 12 inch (30 cm) pizza pan. Sprinkle crust with first amount of cheese.

Combine next 5 ingredients in small bowl. Spoon onto cheese. Spread evenly. Bake in 450°F (230°C) oven for 10 to 15 minutes until crust is crisp and golden.

Arrange tomato slices in single layer over ham mixture.

Combine second amounts of cheese and salad dressing in separate small bowl. Divide and spoon cheese mixture onto each tomato slice. Flatten cheese mixture slightly with back of spoon. Broil 6 inches (15 cm) from heat in oven for 3 to 4 minutes until crust starts to brown and cheese is melted. Cuts into 8 wedges.

1 wedge: 295 Calories; 18 g Total Fat (7.5 g Mono, 3.4 g Poly, 5.2 g Sat); 35 mg Cholesterol; 21 g Carbohydrate; 1 g Fibre; 13 g Protein; 730 mg Sodium

Pictured on page 77.

Kids Can Help

Grating and sprinkling cheese. Stirring ham mixture.

Ham Tomato Pizza, above

Two-Bite Pizzas

*Easy to make, easy to eat! Smoky bacon, mushrooms
and cheese top buttery crescent roll pastry—yum!*

PIZZA TOPPING		
Pizza (or pasta) sauce	1/4 cup	60 mL
Grated part-skim mozzarella cheese	1/4 cup	60 mL
Sliced green onion	2 tbsp.	30 mL
Finely chopped fresh white mushrooms	2 tbsp.	30 mL
Dried basil	1/8 tsp.	0.5 mL
Tube of refrigerator crescent-style rolls (8 rolls per tube)	8 1/2 oz.	235 g
Real (or imitation) bacon bits	2 tbsp.	30 mL

Pizza Topping: Combine first 5 ingredients in small bowl. Makes about 1/2 cup (125 mL) topping.

Remove crescent-style rolls from tube, but don't unroll. Cut into 12 equal slices. Arrange about 2 inches (5 cm) apart on ungreased baking sheet. Flatten each slice into 2 inch (5 cm) diameter disc. Spread about 2 tsp. (10 mL) topping on each disc.

Sprinkle 1/2 tsp. (2 mL) bacon bits evenly over topping on each. Bake in 375°F (190°C) oven for 10 to 12 minutes until edges are golden and cheese is melted. Makes 12 two-bite pizzas.

*1 two-bite pizza: 49 Calories; 2.5 g Total Fat (0.3 g Mono, 0.1 g Poly, 0.3 g Sat); 2 mg Cholesterol;
5 g Carbohydrate; trace Fibre; 2 g Protein; 142 mg Sodium*

Pictured on page 79.

Kids Can Help

Grating cheese. Flattening dough. Putting toppings on pizzas.

Top: Two-Bite Pizzas, above
Bottom: Taco Cheese Swirls, page 80

Taco Cheese Swirls

*These mildly spiced, cheesy biscuits are a tasty alternative
to bread or crackers. Serve with salsa and sour cream.*

All-purpose flour	2 cups	500 mL
Baking powder	4 tsp.	20 mL
Salt	1/4 tsp.	1 mL
Cold hard margarine (or butter), cut up	1/4 cup	60 mL
Milk, approximately	3/4 cup	175 mL
Water, approximately	1 tbsp.	15 mL
Taco seasoning mix, stir before measuring	2 tbsp.	30 mL
Grated medium (or mild) Cheddar cheese	1 cup	250 mL

Combine first 3 ingredients in medium bowl. Cut in margarine until mixture resembles coarse crumbs. Make a well in centre.

Slowly add milk to well, stirring with fork until soft dough forms. Turn out onto lightly floured surface. Knead 6 times. Roll out or press into 10 inch (25 cm) square.

Brush top of dough with water.

Sprinkle taco seasoning evenly over water, leaving 1 1/2 inch (3.8 cm) edge on 1 side. Sprinkle cheese evenly over taco seasoning. Roll up dough, jelly roll-style, toward unsprinkled edge. Press seam against roll to seal. Place, seam-side down, on cutting board. Cut into 10 equal slices. Arrange, cut-side down, about 2 inches (5 cm) apart on parchment paper-lined baking sheet. Bake in 400°F (205°C) oven for 15 to 20 minutes until golden. Freezes well. Makes 10 swirls.

1 swirl: 202 Calories; 9.5 g Total Fat (4.4 g Mono, 0.7 g Poly, 3.7 g Sat); 13 mg Cholesterol; 23 g Carbohydrate; 1 g Fibre; 7 g Protein; 448 mg Sodium

Pictured on page 79.

Kids Can Help

Measuring ingredients. Brushing water on dough.
Grating and sprinkling cheese.

Pizza Dogs

Not your ordinary hot dog! Good warm or cold. Serve with Tropical Hurricane, page 16.

Tube of refrigerator crescent-style rolls (8 rolls per tube)	8 1/2 oz.	235 g
Pizza sauce	1/4 cup	60 mL
Wieners (your favourite)	8	8
Grated part-skim mozzarella cheese	1/2 cup	125 mL

Unroll and separate crescent-style rolls into 8 triangles.

Spread 1 1/2 tsp. (7 mL) pizza sauce on 1 triangle, almost to edges. Place 1 wiener on top of sauce at wide end of triangle. Sprinkle 1 tbsp. (15 mL) cheese over top. Roll up toward point of triangle. Press seam against roll to seal. Repeat with remaining ingredients, for a total of 8 rolls. Arrange rolls evenly spaced apart on greased baking sheet. Bake in 375°F (190°C) oven for about 12 minutes until golden. Freezes well. Makes 8 pizza dogs.

1 pizza dog: 186 Calories; 12.8 g Total Fat (4.7 g Mono, 1 g Poly, 4.1 g Sat); 23 mg Cholesterol; 9 g Carbohydrate; trace Fibre; 7 g Protein; 594 mg Sodium

Pictured above.

Kids Can Help

Spreading pizza sauce. Grating and sprinkling cheese. Rolling up pizza dogs.

Beef And Potato Moons

Flaky pastry turnovers with a hearty steak and potato filling—sure to satisfy any appetite. If desired, omit Flaky Pastry. Use enough pie pastry (your own or a mix) for three single crusts.

FLAKY PASTRY		
All-purpose flour	2 1/2 cups	625 mL
Granulated sugar	1/2 tsp.	2 mL
Salt	1/2 tsp.	2 mL
Cold vegetable shortening, cut up	3/4 cup	175 mL
Egg yolk (large)	1	1
Cold water	5 tbsp.	75 mL
White vinegar	1 tsp.	5 mL
BEEF AND POTATO FILLING		
Inside round steak, diced (see Tip, page 74)	8 oz.	225 g
Finely diced peeled potato	1 cup	250 mL
Finely diced onion	1/2 cup	125 mL
Grated carrot	1/2 cup	125 mL
Ketchup	2 tbsp.	30 mL
Soy sauce	1 tbsp.	15 mL
Worcestershire sauce	1 1/2 tsp.	7 mL
Seasoned salt	1/2 tsp.	2 mL
Pepper	1/4 tsp.	1 mL
Large egg, fork-beaten	1	1

Flaky Pastry - Hand Method: Combine flour, sugar and salt in medium bowl. Cut in shortening until mixture resembles coarse crumbs. Beat egg yolk, water and vinegar with fork in small bowl. Slowly add to flour mixture, stirring with fork until mixture starts to come together. Do not overmix.

Food Processor Method: Process first 4 ingredients until mixture resembles coarse crumbs. Add egg yolk, water and vinegar. Pulse with on/off motion until dough starts to come together. Do not over-process.

Turn out onto lightly floured surface. Press pastry into ball. Flatten slightly into disc. Wrap in plastic wrap. Chill for 30 minutes. Makes about 1 1/4 lbs. (560 g) pastry.

Beef And Potato Filling: Combine first 9 ingredients in large bowl. Makes 2 cups (500 mL) filling. Divide pastry into 6 equal portions. Roll out 1 portion on lightly floured surface to 7 inch (18 cm) circle. Spoon about 1/3 cup (75 mL) filling into centre of circle.

(continued on next page)

Lightly brush edge of circle with egg. Fold pastry over filling. Crimp decorative edge to seal. Repeat with remaining pastry and filling, for a total of 6 turnovers. Arrange in single layer on greased baking sheet. Brush tops and sides of each turnover with egg. Cut small slit in top of each to allow steam to escape. Bake in 400°F (205°C) oven for 20 minutes. Reduce heat to 350°F (175°C). Bake for about 30 minutes until golden. Freezes well. Makes 6 turnovers.

1 turnover: 557 Calories; 31.1 g Total Fat (13 g Mono, 6.3 g Poly, 8.3 g Sat); 88 mg Cholesterol; 51 g Carbohydrate; 3 g Fibre; 17 g Protein; 585 mg Sodium

Pictured below.

Kids Can Help

Cutting in shortening. Peeling and grating carrot. Stirring filling.
Crimping pastry edges to seal. Brushing turnovers with egg.

Pizza Soup

A chunky soup that tastes just like pepperoni pizza!
Freeze individual portions to heat up for a quick lunch.

Cooking oil	2 tsp.	10 mL
Chopped onion	1/2 cup	125 mL
Garlic clove, minced (or 1/4 tsp., 1 mL, powder), optional	1	1
Sliced fresh white mushrooms	1 cup	250 mL
Deli pepperoni slices, each cut into 8 wedges	5 1/2 oz.	154 g
Chopped green pepper	1/2 cup	125 mL
Cans of diced tomatoes (14 oz., 398 mL, each), with juice	2	2
Prepared beef broth	1 cup	250 mL
Dried basil	1/2 tsp.	2 mL
Grated part-skim mozzarella cheese, for garnish		

Heat cooking oil in large saucepan on medium. Add onion and garlic. Cook for about 2 minutes, stirring often, until onion starts to soften.

Add mushrooms, pepperoni and green pepper. Cook for about 5 minutes, stirring occasionally, until green pepper is softened.

Add next 3 ingredients. Stir. Bring to a boil on medium-high. Reduce heat to medium-low. Simmer, uncovered, for about 10 minutes.

Garnish individual servings with cheese. Freezes well. Makes about 5 cups (1.25 L).

1 cup (250 mL): 206 Calories; 15 g Total Fat (7.2 g Mono, 2 g Poly, 4.9 g Sat); 23 mg Cholesterol; 10 g Carbohydrate; 2 g Fibre; 9 g Protein; 993 mg Sodium

Pictured on page 85.

Kids Can Help

Slicing mushrooms and pepperoni. Grating cheese.

Top: Oodles Of Noodles, page 86
Centre: Taco Chicken Soup, page 87
Bottom: Pizza Soup, above

Oodles Of Noodles

A bowl full of noodles makes a quick lunch. Chicken and vegetables make this tasty soup filling and nutritious.

Cooking oil	2 tsp.	10 mL
Boneless, skinless chicken breast halves, chopped	8 oz.	225 g
Package of instant noodles with chicken-flavoured seasoning	3 oz.	85 g
Water	2 cups	500 mL
Prepared chicken broth	1 cup	250 mL
Can of kernel corn, drained	7 oz.	199 mL
Chopped broccoli (optional)	1/2 cup	125 mL
Chopped green onion	3 tbsp.	50 mL

Heat cooking oil in large saucepan on medium. Add chicken. Cook for about 10 minutes, stirring occasionally, until chicken is no longer pink.

Break up noodles. Add noodles with seasoning and remaining 5 ingredients to chicken. Stir. Bring to a boil on medium-high. Reduce heat to medium-low. Cover. Simmer for about 2 minutes until noodles are tender but firm. Soup may be frozen, but noodles will absorb broth and soften. Makes about 5 cups (1.25 L).

1 cup (250 mL): 178 Calories; 3.6 g Total Fat (1.6 g Mono, 1 g Poly, 0.6 g Sat); 33 mg Cholesterol; 19 g Carbohydrate; 1 g Fibre; 17 g Protein; 380 mg Sodium

Pictured on page 85.

Kids Can Help

Washing vegetables. Breaking noodles.
Adding seasoning and corn to saucepan.

Taco Chicken Soup

For taco fans of all ages—sure to be a hit!
Take to school in a thermos with a bag of tortilla chips.

Bacon slices, diced	2	2
Sliced fresh white mushrooms	1 cup	250 mL
Chopped onion	2/3 cup	150 mL
Chopped red pepper	1/2 cup	125 mL
Prepared chicken broth	4 cups	1 L
Chopped cooked chicken	2 cups	500 mL
Can of kernel corn, drained	12 oz.	341 mL
Jar of mild taco sauce	7 1/2 oz.	215 mL
Salt	1/4 tsp.	1 mL
Grated medium (or mild) Cheddar cheese, for garnish		

Cook bacon in large saucepan on medium until almost crisp. Do not drain.

Add next 3 ingredients. Cook for 5 to 10 minutes, stirring often, until onion is softened.

Add next 5 ingredients. Stir. Bring to a boil. Reduce heat to medium-low. Cover. Simmer for about 10 minutes until chicken is heated through.

Garnish individual servings with cheese. Freezes well. Makes about 8 cups (2 L).

1 cup (250 mL): 148 Calories; 4.6 g Total Fat (1.8 g Mono, 1 g Poly, 1.3 g Sat); 35 mg Cholesterol; 12 g Carbohydrate; 2 g Fibre; 16 g Protein; 721 mg Sodium

Pictured on page 85.

Kids Can Help

Washing vegetables. Slicing mushrooms. Measuring chicken broth.

Hamburger Soup

Tender vegetables and a robust tomato herb broth transform hamburger into a marvelous midday meal, ready in minutes!

Cooking oil	1 tsp.	5 mL
Lean ground beef	1 lb.	454 g
Chopped onion	1 cup	250 mL
Diced carrot	1 cup	250 mL
Chopped celery	1/2 cup	125 mL
Can of diced tomatoes (with juice)	14 oz.	398 mL
Water	1 1/2 cups	375 mL
Can of condensed beef broth	10 oz.	284 mL
Frozen kernel corn	1 cup	250 mL
Can of tomato sauce	7 1/2 oz.	213 mL
Granulated sugar	1 tsp.	5 mL
Worcestershire sauce	1 tsp.	5 mL
Dried basil (optional)	1/2 – 1 tsp.	2 – 5 mL
Pepper	1/4 tsp.	1 mL

Heat cooking oil in large saucepan on medium. Add ground beef. Scramble-fry for about 5 minutes until no longer pink. Drain.

Add onion, carrot and celery. Cook for about 5 minutes, stirring often, until onion is softened.

Add remaining 9 ingredients. Stir. Bring to a boil on medium-high. Reduce heat to medium-low. Cover. Simmer for about 45 minutes until vegetables are tender. Freezes well. Makes about 6 3/4 cups (1.7 L).

1 cup (250 mL): 183 Calories; 6.9 g Total Fat (3 g Mono, 0.6 g Poly, 2.4 g Sat); 35 mg Cholesterol; 16 g Carbohydrate; 3 g Fibre; 16 g Protein; 634 mg Sodium

Pictured on page 91.

Kids Can Help

Washing vegetables. Peeling carrots. Measuring corn.

Chicken Pasta Soup

This recipe will become your own as you try mixing and matching pasta and vegetables. A great way to use leftovers. Never the same twice!

Cooking oil	1 tbsp.	15 mL
Sliced fresh white mushrooms	1 1/2 cups	375 mL
Chopped onion	1 cup	250 mL
Garlic clove, minced (or 1/4 tsp., 1 mL, powder), optional	1	1
Prepared chicken broth	6 cups	1.5 L
Chopped cooked chicken	1 1/2 cups	375 mL
Cooked pasta (about 1/2 cup, 125 mL, uncooked)	1 cup	250 mL
Frozen mixed vegetables, thawed (or cooked vegetables)	1 1/2 cups	375 mL

Heat cooking oil in large saucepan on medium. Add mushrooms and onion. Cook for 5 to 10 minutes, stirring often, until onion is softened.

Add garlic. Heat and stir for 1 to 2 minutes until fragrant.

Add next 3 ingredients. Stir. Bring to a boil. Reduce heat to medium-low. Simmer, uncovered, for 5 minutes.

Add mixed vegetables. Heat and stir for about 5 minutes until vegetables are cooked or heated through. May be frozen, but pasta will absorb broth and soften. Makes about 8 1/2 cups (2.1 L).

1 cup (250 mL): 151 Calories; 5 g Total Fat (2.1 g Mono, 1.3 g Poly, 1 g Sat); 24 mg Cholesterol; 13 g Carbohydrate; 2 g Fibre; 14 g Protein; 619 mg Sodium

Pictured on page 91.

Kids Can Help

Slicing mushrooms. Measuring pasta and frozen vegetables.

ABC Soup

Kids will enjoy this fun-filled chicken soup. Add diced cooked chicken when you have leftovers. Serve with breadsticks.

Cooking oil	2 tsp.	10 mL
Chopped onion	1/2 cup	125 mL
Diced carrot	1/2 cup	125 mL
Chopped celery	1/2 cup	125 mL
Water	4 cups	1 L
Cans of condensed chicken broth (10 oz., 284 mL, each)	2	2
Bay leaf	1	1
Parsley flakes	1 tsp.	5 mL
Dried thyme	1/2 tsp.	2 mL
Alphabet pasta	1/2 cup	125 mL
Frozen California mixed vegetables, partially thawed, chopped	1 cup	250 mL

Heat cooking oil in large saucepan on medium. Add onion, carrot and celery. Cook for 5 to 10 minutes, stirring often, until onion is softened.

Add next 5 ingredients. Stir. Bring to a boil on medium-high.

Add pasta. Stir. Reduce heat to medium-low. Cover. Simmer for about 8 minutes until pasta is tender but firm.

Add mixed vegetables. Bring to a boil on medium-high. Reduce heat to medium-low. Cover. Simmer for 1 to 2 minutes until vegetables are cooked. Discard bay leaf. May be frozen, but pasta will absorb broth and soften. Makes about 7 3/4 cups (1.9 L).

1 cup (250 mL): 95 Calories; 2.3 g Total Fat (1.1 g Mono, 0.7 g Poly, 0.4 g Sat); 1 mg Cholesterol; 13 g Carbohydrate; 2 g Fibre; 6 g Protein; 514 mg Sodium

Pictured on page 91.

Kids Can Help

Washing vegetables. Peeling carrots. Measuring pasta.

Top: ABC Soup, above
Centre: Hamburger Soup, page 88
Bottom: Chicken Pasta Soup, page 89

Mushroom Rice Soup

You won't need a lot of "thyme" to create this delectable soup the whole family will love! Serve with a salad or buns.

Water	4 cups	1 L
Can of sliced mushrooms (with liquid)	10 oz.	284 mL
Can of condensed cream of mushroom soup	10 oz.	284 mL
Chopped onion	1/2 cup	125 mL
Thinly sliced carrot	1/3 cup	75 mL
Celery rib, thinly sliced	1	1
Chicken bouillon powder	1 tbsp.	15 mL
Parsley flakes	1 1/2 tsp.	7 mL
Dried thyme	1/4 – 1/2 tsp.	1 – 2 mL
Pepper	1/8 tsp.	0.5 mL
Long grain white rice	1/2 cup	125 mL

Combine first 10 ingredients in large saucepan. Bring to a boil on medium-high.

Add rice. Stir. Reduce heat to medium-low. Simmer, uncovered, for 20 to 30 minutes until rice is tender. Freezes well. Makes about 6 1/2 cups (1.6 L).

1 cup (250 mL): 122 Calories; 4 g Total Fat (0.8 g Mono, 1.8 g Poly, 1.1 g Sat); 1 mg Cholesterol; 19 g Carbohydrate; 1 g Fibre; 3 g Protein; 780 mg Sodium

Pictured on page 93.

Kids Can Help

Washing vegetables. Peeling carrot. Measuring rice.

Tuna Corn Chowder

A simple can of tuna turns corn chowder into a complete meal.

Hard margarine (or butter)	1 tbsp.	15 mL
Chopped onion	1/3 cup	75 mL
Chopped celery	1/4 cup	60 mL

(continued on next page)

Water	1 1/2 cups	375 mL
Diced peeled potato	1 cup	250 mL
Chicken bouillon powder	1 tsp.	5 mL
Dill weed	1/2 tsp.	2 mL
Salt	1/2 tsp.	2 mL
Pepper	1/4 tsp.	1 mL
Can of cream-style corn	14 oz.	398 mL
Milk	1 cup	250 mL
Can of flaked tuna, drained	6 oz.	170 g

Melt margarine in large saucepan on medium. Add onion and celery. Cook for 5 to 10 minutes, stirring often, until onion is softened.

Add next 6 ingredients. Stir. Bring to a boil on medium-high. Reduce heat to medium-low. Cover. Simmer for about 10 minutes until potato is tender.

Add corn, milk and tuna. Heat for about 10 minutes, stirring occasionally, until heated through. Do not boil. Freezes well. Makes about 5 cups (1.25 L).

1 cup (250 mL): 176 Calories; 4.3 g Total Fat (2.1 g Mono, 0.8 g Poly, 1.2 g Sat); 15 mg Cholesterol; 25 g Carbohydrate; 2 g Fibre; 11 g Protein; 787 mg Sodium

Pictured below.

Kids Can Help

Washing vegetables. Measuring water. Peeling potato.

Left: Mushroom Rice Soup, page 92   Right: Tuna Corn Chowder, page 92

Tomato Beef Stew

A hint of rosemary adds a perfect touch to tangy tomato and tender beef stew. Recipe may be doubled for a family meal.

All-purpose flour	2 tbsp.	30 mL
Beef stew meat, cut into 1/2 inch (12 mm) cubes	3/4 lb.	340 g
Cooking oil	1 tbsp.	15 mL
Cooking oil	2 tsp.	10 mL
Chopped onion	1/2 cup	125 mL
Chopped celery	1/2 cup	125 mL
Can of diced tomatoes (with juice)	14 oz.	398 mL
Prepared beef broth	1/2 cup	125 mL
Ketchup	2 tbsp.	30 mL
Worcestershire sauce	1 tsp.	5 mL
Dried rosemary, crushed	1/2 tsp.	2 mL
Salt	1/8 tsp.	0.5 mL

Measure flour into medium resealable freezer bag. Add beef. Seal bag. Toss until coated.

Heat first amount of cooking oil in large saucepan on medium-high. Add beef. Cook for about 5 minutes, stirring occasionally, until browned on all sides. Transfer to large bowl.

Heat second amount of cooking oil in same saucepan on medium. Add onion and celery. Cook for 5 to 10 minutes, stirring often, until onion is softened.

Add beef and remaining 6 ingredients. Stir. Bring to a boil. Reduce heat to medium-low. Cover. Simmer for about 1 hour, stirring occasionally, until beef is tender. Remove cover. Simmer for about 15 minutes until sauce is thickened. Freezes well. Makes about 3 cups (750 mL).

1 cup (250 mL): 336 Calories; 18.1 g Total Fat (8.8 g Mono, 2.9 g Poly, 4.6 g Sat); 63 mg Cholesterol; 16 g Carbohydrate; 2 g Fibre; 28 g Protein; 687 mg Sodium

Pictured on page 95.

Kids Can Help

Tossing freezer bag to coat beef. Washing celery.

Left: Tomato Beef Stew, above
Right: Pork And Bean Melt, page 96

Pork And Bean Melt

Kid-friendly baked beans with chunks of sausage and melted cheese.

Cooking oil	1 tsp.	5 mL
Pork breakfast sausages	8	8
Can of baked beans in tomato sauce	14 oz.	398 mL
White vinegar	1 tbsp.	15 mL
Brown sugar, packed	1 tsp.	5 mL
Grated medium (or mild) Cheddar cheese	1/4 cup	60 mL
Grated part-skim mozzarella cheese	1/4 cup	60 mL

Heat cooking oil in large frying pan on medium until hot. Add sausages. Cook for 10 to 12 minutes, turning occasionally, until no longer pink inside. Remove from heat. Cut sausages into 1 inch (2.5 cm) pieces. Return to frying pan.

Add baked beans, vinegar and brown sugar. Stir well. Spread evenly in pan.

Sprinkle both cheeses over top. Cover. Heat on medium-low for 2 to 3 minutes until cheese is melted. Makes about 2 cups (500 mL).

1/2 cup (125 mL): 330 Calories; 20 g Total Fat (8.4 g Mono, 2.4 g Poly, 8.2 g Sat); 49 mg Cholesterol; 25 g Carbohydrate; 8 g Fibre; 15 g Protein; 884 mg Sodium

Pictured on page 95.

Kids Can Help

Opening can. Grating cheeses.

Creamy Chicken Stew

Chunks of chicken and vegetables in a well-seasoned sauce.
This recipe is easily doubled for a family meal.

Cooking oil	2 tsp.	10 mL
Boneless, skinless chicken thighs, cubed	1 lb.	454 g
Chopped onion	1/2 cup	125 mL
Chopped carrot	1/2 cup	125 mL
All-purpose flour	1 tbsp.	15 mL
Prepared chicken broth	1 cup	250 mL
Bacon slices, cooked crisp and crumbled	3	3
Salt	1/4 tsp.	1 mL
Pepper	1/8 tsp.	0.5 mL
Frozen peas	1/3 cup	75 mL
Sour cream	2 tbsp.	30 mL

Heat cooking oil in large saucepan on medium. Add chicken. Cook for about 10 minutes, stirring occasionally, until no longer pink inside.

Add onion and carrot. Cook for 5 to 10 minutes, stirring often, until onion is softened.

Add flour. Heat and stir for 1 minute.

Slowly add broth, stirring constantly. Add bacon, salt and pepper. Heat and stir until boiling and thickened. Reduce heat to medium-low. Cover. Simmer for about 15 minutes until carrot is tender.

Add peas and sour cream. Stir. Cover. Cook for about 5 minutes until peas are tender. Makes about 2 1/2 cups (625 mL).

1/2 cup (125 mL): 201 Calories; 9.8 g Total Fat (3.9 g Mono, 2.1 g Poly, 2.7 g Sat); 81 mg Cholesterol; 6 g Carbohydrate; 1 g Fibre; 21 g Protein; 369 mg Sodium

Pictured on page 99.

Kids Can Help

Crumbling bacon. Peeling carrots. Measuring peas and sour cream.

Mexi-Chili

Yummy Tex-Mex beef and bean combo kids will love! Serve with corn chips.

Cooking oil	2 tsp.	10 mL
Lean ground beef	1 lb.	454 g
Chopped onion	1 1/2 cups	375 mL
Envelope of taco seasoning mix	1 1/4 oz.	35 g
Cans of red kidney beans (14 oz., 398 mL, each), rinsed and drained	2	2
Chopped tomato	3 cups	750 mL
Sour cream	1/3 cup	75 mL
Sliced green onion	3 tbsp.	50 mL

Heat cooking oil in large frying pan on medium. Add ground beef and onion. Scramble-fry for 5 to 10 minutes until beef is no longer pink.

Add next 3 ingredients. Heat and stir for about 5 minutes until thickened.

Add sour cream and green onion. Heat and stir for 1 to 2 minutes until heated through. Freezes well. Makes about 6 cups (1.5 L).

1 cup (250 mL): 343 Calories; 16.1 g Total Fat (6.7 g Mono, 1.4 g Poly, 6.1 g Sat); 48 mg Cholesterol; 28 g Carbohydrate; 7 g Fibre; 23 g Protein; 572 mg Sodium

Pictured on page 99.

Kids Can Help

Opening cans. Measuring sour cream. Washing green onion.

Top: Creamy Chicken Stew, page 97
Bottom: Mexi-Chili, above

Coconut Apricot Logs

An attractive treat everyone will love. Delicious right out of the freezer!

Can of sweetened condensed milk	11 oz.	300 mL
Hard margarine (or butter)	1/2 cup	125 mL
Brown sugar, packed	1/3 cup	75 mL
White chocolate baking squares (1 oz., 28 g, each), chopped	6	6
Graham cracker crumbs	1 1/3 cups	325 mL
Finely chopped dried apricot	1 cup	250 mL
Medium unsweetened coconut	3/4 cup	175 mL

Combine first 3 ingredients in heavy medium saucepan. Heat and stir on medium until margarine is melted.

Add chocolate. Heat and stir on lowest heat until almost melted. Do not overheat. Remove from heat. Stir until smooth.

Add graham crumbs and apricot. Stir well. Press firmly in greased 9 x 13 inch (22 x 33 cm) pan. Cover. Chill for about 3 hours until firm. Invert onto cutting board. Cut into 8 rows lengthwise and 8 rows crosswise, for a total of 64 pieces. Roll 1 piece into 2 inch (5 cm) long log.

Roll in coconut in shallow dish until coated. Repeat with remaining pieces and coconut. Arrange logs on waxed paper-lined baking sheet. Chill for at least 1 hour until firm. Freezes well. Makes 64 logs.

1 log: 72 Calories; 3.8 g Total Fat (1.5 g Mono, 0.2 g Poly, 1.8 g Sat); 3 mg Cholesterol; 9 g Carbohydrate; trace Fibre; 1 g Protein; 40 mg Sodium

Pictured on page 101.

Kids Can Help

Counting chocolate baking squares. Measuring dry ingredients.
Rolling logs in coconut.

Top Right: Presto Cookies, page 102
Bottom Left: Coconut Apricot Logs, above

Chewy Oaty Bars

Quick and easy to make. Rolled oats and coconut are naturally delicious.

Quick-cooking rolled oats (not instant)	1 cup	250 mL
All-purpose flour	1 cup	250 mL
Medium unsweetened coconut	2/3 cup	150 mL
Brown sugar, packed	1/2 cup	125 mL
Hard margarine (or butter)	1/2 cup	125 mL
Golden corn syrup	3 tbsp.	50 mL
Water	1 tbsp.	15 mL
Baking soda	1/2 tsp.	2 mL

Combine first 4 ingredients in large bowl.

Measure margarine, corn syrup and water into medium saucepan. Heat and stir on medium until margarine is melted. Remove from heat.

Add baking soda. Stir well. Add to rolled oats mixture. Mix well. Press firmly in greased 9 × 9 inch (22 × 22 cm) pan. Bake in 325°F (160°C) oven for about 20 minutes until set and golden. Cool. Store in airtight container. Freezes well. Cuts into 18 bars.

1 bar: 154 Calories; 8.1 g Total Fat (3.7 g Mono, 0.7 g Poly, 3.2 g Sat); 0 mg Cholesterol; 19 g Carbohydrate; 1 g Fibre; 2 g Protein; 107 mg Sodium

Pictured on page 103.

Kids Can Help

Measuring dry ingredients. Stirring.

Presto Cookies

A delightful crispy-crunch in a buttery cookie. Dough may be rolled, wrapped and frozen for quick slicing and baking another day. Presto!

Icing (confectioner's) sugar	1 1/2 cups	375 mL
Hard margarine (or butter), softened	1 cup	250 mL
Vanilla	1 1/2 tsp.	7 mL
Large eggs	2	2

(continued on next page)

All-purpose flour	2 3/4 cups	675 mL
Coarsely crushed cornflakes cereal	2 cups	500 mL
Medium sweetened coconut, toasted	3/4 cup	175 mL
(see Tip, page 34)		

Beat icing sugar, margarine and vanilla in large bowl until smooth. Add eggs, 1 at a time, beating well after each addition.

Add flour. Mix well. Add cereal and coconut. Mix. Divide dough into 3 equal portions. Roll each portion into 2 inch (5 cm) diameter log. Wrap each log in waxed paper. Fold ends under to enclose. Place logs in large resealable freezer bag or airtight container. Chill for 2 hours (see Note). Cut 1 log into 1/4 inch (6 mm) slices with serrated knife. Arrange about 1/2 inch (12 mm) apart on greased cookie sheet. Bake in 350°F (175°C) oven for about 12 minutes until golden. Repeat with remaining logs. Makes 6 dozen (72) cookies.

1 cookie: 69 Calories; 3.1 g Total Fat (1.8 g Mono, 0.3 g Poly, 0.8 g Sat); 6 mg Cholesterol; 9 g Carbohydrate; trace Fibre; 1 g Protein; 62 mg Sodium

Pictured on page 101.

Note: Logs freeze well. To serve, thaw frozen log in refrigerator overnight. Cut with serrated knife for best results.

Kids Can Help

Measuring dry ingredients. Crushing cereal. Rolling and wrapping dough. Arranging slices on cookie sheet.

Chewy Oaty Bars, page 102

Hit-The-Trail Mix

A surprise in every handful! Best eaten within a day or two, when popcorn is fresh. Pack this in their lunch on a field trip day.

Popped corn (about 3 tbsp., 50 mL, unpopped)	4 cups	1 L
Whole wheat squares cereal	2 cups	500 mL
Hard margarine (or butter), melted	1/4 cup	60 mL
Grated Parmesan cheese	2 tbsp.	30 mL
Seasoned salt	1 – 2 tsp.	5 – 10 mL
Dark raisins	1/2 cup	125 mL
Quartered dried apricot	1/2 cup	125 mL
Chopped dried apple	1/2 cup	125 mL
Box of candy-coated chocolate candies (such as Smarties or M & M's)	2 oz.	56 g

Measure popped corn and cereal into large bowl. Stir well.

Combine next 3 ingredients in 2 cup (500 mL) liquid measure. Drizzle over popcorn mixture. Toss until coated. Spread evenly in ungreased baking sheet with sides. Bake in 300°F (150°C) oven for about 10 minutes until crisp and lightly browned. Cool. Transfer to same large bowl.

Add remaining 4 ingredients. Mix well. Makes about 7 cups (1.75 L).

1 cup (250 mL): 245 Calories; 9.7 g Total Fat (4.7 g Mono, 0.9 g Poly, 1.7 g Sat); 2 mg Cholesterol; 39 g Carbohydrate; 4 g Fibre; 4 g Protein; 389 mg Sodium

Pictured on front cover.

Kids Can Help

Grating Parmesan cheese. Measuring dry ingredients.
Tossing popcorn mixture.

Honey Crisp Bars

So crunchy and sweet—these won't last long!

Hard margarine (or butter)	3/4 cup	175 mL
Instant chocolate drink powder	2/3 cup	150 mL
Liquid honey	1/3 cup	75 mL

(continued on next page)

Crisp rice cereal	2 cups	500 mL
Cornflakes cereal	1 2/3 cups	400 mL
Graham cracker crumbs	2/3 cup	150 mL
Medium sweetened coconut	1/2 cup	125 mL

Combine first 3 ingredients in large saucepan. Heat and stir on medium until margarine is melted. Remove from heat.

Add remaining 4 ingredients. Mix well. Press firmly in greased 9 × 13 inch (22 × 33 cm) pan. Cover. Chill for about 1 hour until firm. Cut into 6 rows lengthwise and 8 rows crosswise, for a total of 4 dozen (48) bars.

1 bar: 62 Calories; 3.5 g Total Fat (2.1 g Mono, 0.3 g Poly, 0.9 g Sat); 0 mg Cholesterol; 8 g Carbohydrate; trace Fibre; 0 g Protein; 72 mg Sodium

Pictured above.

Kids Can Help

Measuring dry ingredients. Pressing mixture in pan.

Pineapple Pudding Dip

Kids will love this as a dip for fresh fruit or as a dessert all by itself. Be sure to send along a spoon! Can be made ahead and frozen in individual airtight containers.

Can of crushed pineapple (with juice)	14 oz.	398 mL
Box of instant vanilla pudding powder (4 serving size)	1	1
Milk	1/2 cup	125 mL
Frozen whipped topping, thawed	1 cup	250 mL

Process first 3 ingredients in blender or food processor until smooth. Transfer to medium bowl.

Fold in whipped topping. Makes about 3 1/2 cups (875 mL).

1/2 cup (125 mL): 133 Calories; 3.2 g Total Fat (0.3 g Mono, 0.1 g Poly, 2.6 g Sat); 1 mg Cholesterol; 26 g Carbohydrate; 1 g Fibre; 1 g Protein; 223 mg Sodium

Pictured on page 107.

Kids Can Help

Measuring ingredients. Stirring.

Oatmeal Dippers

Delightfully crunchy oatmeal and coconut cookies. Dip into Pineapple Pudding Dip, above, or Apple Cinnamon Dip, page 113.

Hard margarine (or butter), softened	1/2 cup	125 mL
Brown sugar, packed	1/2 cup	125 mL
Large egg	1	1
Vanilla	1 tsp.	5 mL
Quick-cooking rolled oats (not instant)	1 cup	250 mL
Whole wheat flour	1/2 cup	125 mL
Medium sweetened coconut	1/2 cup	125 mL
Natural oat bran	1/4 cup	60 mL
Baking soda	1/2 tsp.	2 mL
Ground cinnamon	1/2 tsp.	2 mL
Salt	1/4 tsp.	1 mL

(continued on next page)

Cream margarine and brown sugar in large bowl. Add egg and vanilla. Mix well.

Combine remaining 7 ingredients in medium bowl. Add to margarine mixture. Mix well. Press evenly in waxed paper-lined 8 x 8 inch (20 x 20 cm) pan. Chill for 1 hour. Invert onto cutting board. Discard waxed paper. Cut rolled oats mixture in half. Cut each half crosswise into 12 pieces, for a total of 24 pieces. Arrange about 1 inch (2.5 cm) apart on greased cookie sheets. Bake in 350°F (175°C) oven for about 10 minutes until golden. Let stand on cookie sheets for 5 minutes before removing to wire racks to cool. Makes 2 dozen (24) cookies.

1 cookie: 94 Calories; 5.2 g Total Fat (2.9 g Mono, 0.6 g Poly, 1.4 g Sat); 9 mg Cholesterol; 11 g Carbohydrate; 1 g Fibre; 2 g Protein; 108 mg Sodium

Pictured below.

Kids Can Help

Measuring dry ingredients. Beating egg. Stirring.

Left: Oatmeal Dippers, page 106
Right: Pineapple Pudding Dip, page 106

Bacon Cheese Spread

A nice addition to any lunch bag. Serve with your favourite crackers.

Grated medium Cheddar cheese	1/2 cup	125 mL
Vegetable spreadable cream cheese	1/4 cup	60 mL
Finely diced green pepper (optional)	1 tbsp.	15 mL
Finely diced green onion	1 tbsp.	15 mL
Real (or imitation) bacon bits	1 tbsp.	15 mL

Combine all 5 ingredients in small bowl. Makes about 1/2 cup (125 mL).

1 tsp. (5 mL): 19 Calories; 1.7 g Total Fat (0.5 g Mono, 0.1 g Poly, 1.1 g Sat); 5 mg Cholesterol; 0 g Carbohydrate; trace Fibre; 1 g Protein; 24 mg Sodium

Pictured on page 109.

Kids Can Help

Grating cheese. Washing vegetables. Measuring bacon bits.

Avocado Ranch Spuds

Lightly seasoned, golden potato wedges and a tangy avocado dip.

Medium potato (with skin)	1	1
Cooking oil	1/2 tsp.	2 mL
Seasoned salt, sprinkle		
AVOCADO RANCH DIP		
Mashed ripe avocado	1/3 cup	75 mL
Ranch-style dressing	1 tbsp.	15 mL
Sour cream	1 tbsp.	15 mL
Lemon juice	1 tsp.	5 mL
Salt, sprinkle		
Pepper, sprinkle		

Cut potato in half lengthwise. Cut each half lengthwise into 4 wedges. Transfer to large bowl.

Combine cooking oil and seasoned salt in small cup. Drizzle over potato wedges. Toss until coated. Arrange potato wedges on greased baking sheet. Bake in 350°F (175°C) oven for about 45 minutes, turning occasionally, until golden.

(continued on next page)

Avocado Ranch Dip: Combine all 6 ingredients in small bowl. Makes about 1/2 cup (125 mL) dip. Serve with potato wedges. Serves 2.

1 serving: 175 Calories; 11.7 g Total Fat (4.9 g Mono, 1.2 g Poly, 2.3 g Sat); 4 mg Cholesterol; 16 g Carbohydrate; 2 g Fibre; 3 g Protein; 105 mg Sodium

Pictured below.

Kids Can Help

Mashing avocado. Stirring.

Top Left: Avocado Ranch Dip, page 108
Top Right: Avocado Ranch Spuds, page 108
Bottom Right: Bacon Cheese Spread, page 108

Banana Bread Dunkers

Enjoy a chat with your kids. Give them a glass of milk, make yourself something hot to drink and dunk together! Try with Apple Cinnamon Dip, page 113.

Brown sugar, packed	1/3 cup	75 mL
Hard margarine (or butter), softened	1/4 cup	60 mL
Large eggs	2	2
Egg white (large)	1	1
Vanilla	1 tsp.	5 mL
Mashed banana (about 1 large)	1/2 cup	125 mL
All-purpose flour	2 cups	500 mL
Whole wheat flour	1/2 cup	125 mL
Baking soda	1 tsp.	5 mL
Salt	1/4 tsp.	1 mL

Beat first 5 ingredients in large bowl until thick and creamy. Add banana. Beat well.

Add remaining 4 ingredients. Mix well. Turn out onto lightly floured surface. Knead 6 times. Roll into 16 inch (40 cm) long log, about 3 1/2 inches (9 cm) in diameter. Place on greased baking sheet. Bake in 350°F (175°C) oven for 30 minutes. Let stand on baking sheet on wire rack for about 15 minutes until cool enough to handle. Cut log diagonally into 1/2 inch (12 mm) thick slices. Cut each slice in half. Arrange evenly spaced apart on 2 ungreased baking sheets. Bake on separate racks in 275°F (140°C) oven for 10 minutes, switching position of pans at halftime. Turn slices over. Turn oven off. Let stand in oven for about 30 minutes until crisp. Cool. Store in airtight container. Makes about 4 dozen (48) dunkers.

1 dunker: 46 Calories; 1.3 g Total Fat (0.8 g Mono, 0.2 g Poly, 0.3 g Sat); 9 mg Cholesterol; 7 g Carbohydrate; trace Fibre; 1 g Protein; 56 mg Sodium

Pictured on front cover.

Kids Can Help

Mashing banana. Measuring dry ingredients.
Arranging pieces on baking sheet.

Left: Sprinkle Cookies, page 112   Right: Tangy Pineapple Dip, below

Tangy Pineapple Dip

*Maple and cinnamon add a sweet 'n' spicy touch
to this chunky yogurt dip. Great with fresh fruit.*

Plain yogurt	2/3 cup	150 mL
Finely chopped (or crushed) canned pineapple, drained	1/4 cup	60 mL
Maple (or maple-flavoured) syrup	3 tbsp.	50 mL
Ground cinnamon, sprinkle		

Combine all 4 ingredients in small bowl. Makes about 1 cup (250 mL).

1/2 cup (125 mL): 143 Calories; 1.4 g Total Fat (0.4 g Mono, 0.1 g Poly, 0.9 g Sat); 5 mg Cholesterol; 29 g Carbohydrate; trace Fibre; 5 g Protein; 64 mg Sodium

Pictured above.

Kids Can Help

Measuring ingredients. Stirring.

Sprinkle Cookies

Bright and colourful. Scrumptious cookies with a light lemon glaze.

Brown sugar, packed	2/3 cup	150 mL
Large egg	1	1
Cooking oil	1/4 cup	60 mL
Vanilla	1/2 tsp.	2 mL
All-purpose flour	3/4 cup	175 mL
Quick-cooking rolled oats (not instant)	1/3 cup	75 mL
Baking powder	1 tsp.	5 mL
Baking soda	1/4 tsp.	1 mL
LEMON GLAZE		
Icing (confectioner's) sugar	3/4 cup	175 mL
Milk	1 tbsp.	15 mL
Lemon juice	2 tsp.	10 mL
Hard margarine (or butter)	2 tsp.	10 mL
Drops of yellow liquid food colouring	1 – 2	1 – 2
Candy sprinkles	1/2 cup	125 mL

Beat brown sugar and egg in medium bowl until thick and pale. Add cooking oil and vanilla. Beat well.

Combine next 4 ingredients in small bowl. Add to brown sugar mixture. Mix well. Cover. Chill for 1 to 2 hours until just firm. Roll dough into balls, using 1 tbsp. (15 mL) for each. Arrange balls about 2 inches (5 cm) apart on greased cookie sheets. Bake in 375°F (190°C) oven for 8 to 10 minutes until golden. Let stand on cookie sheets for 5 minutes before removing to wire racks to cool.

Lemon Glaze: Combine first 4 ingredients in small saucepan. Heat and stir on medium for about 3 minutes until smooth. Remove from heat. Let stand for about 5 minutes until slightly thickened.

Add food colouring. Stir well. Spread 1 tsp. (5 mL) glaze on each cookie.

Measure candy sprinkles into shallow dish. Dip cookies, glaze-side down, into sprinkles. Let stand, glaze-side up, on wire rack for about 30 minutes until glaze is set. Store in airtight container. Makes 1 1/2 dozen (18) cookies.

1 cookie: 161 Calories; 4.1 g Total Fat (2.3 g Mono, 1.1 g Poly, 0.4 g Sat); 12 mg Cholesterol; 31 g Carbohydrate; trace Fibre; 1 g Protein; 55 mg Sodium

Pictured on page 111 and on back cover.

(continued on next page)

Kids Can Help

Measuring dry ingredients. Rolling dough into balls.
Dipping glazed cookies in sprinkles.

Apple Cinnamon Dip

A smooth and creamy dip that clings to fresh fruit.
Serve with Banana Bread Dunkers, page 110.

Block of cream cheese, softened	8 oz.	250 g
Applesauce	1/4 cup	60 mL
Icing (confectioner's) sugar	3 tbsp.	50 mL
Apple juice	2 tbsp.	30 mL
Milk	2 tbsp.	30 mL
Ground cinnamon	1/2 tsp.	2 mL

Beat all 6 ingredients in medium bowl until smooth. Makes about 2 cups
(500 mL).

1/2 cup (125 mL): 255 Calories; 21.9 g Total Fat (6.2 g Mono, 0.8 g Poly, 13.8 g Sat); 69 mg Cholesterol;
11 g Carbohydrate; trace Fibre; 5 g Protein; 189 mg Sodium

Pictured on front cover.

Apple Blueberry Muffins

Golden and tender, these fruit-filled muffins are a tasty take-to-school treat that will satisfy hunger any time of day!

All-purpose flour	2 cups	500 mL
Brown sugar, packed	3/4 cup	175 mL
Baking powder	1 tbsp.	15 mL
Ground cinnamon	1/2 tsp.	2 mL
Salt	1/4 tsp.	1 mL
Milk	3/4 cup	175 mL
Applesauce	1/3 cup	75 mL
Large egg	1	1
Cooking oil	3 tbsp.	50 mL
Fresh (or frozen, thawed) blueberries	3/4 cup	175 mL
Small cooking apple (such as McIntosh), peeled and core removed, diced (about 3/4 cup, 175 mL)	1	1

Combine first 5 ingredients in large bowl. Make a well in centre.

Beat next 4 ingredients with whisk in small bowl. Add to well.

Add blueberries and apple. Stir until just moistened. Spray 12 muffin cups with cooking spray. Fill cups 3/4 full. Bake in 375°F (190°C) oven for 15 to 20 minutes until wooden pick inserted in centre of muffin comes out clean. Let stand in pan for 5 minutes before removing to wire rack to cool. Freezes well. Makes 1 dozen (12) muffins.

1 muffin: 194 Calories; 4.3 g Total Fat (2.3 g Mono, 1.2 g Poly, 0.5 g Sat); 19 mg Cholesterol; 36 g Carbohydrate; 1 g Fibre; 3 g Protein; 162 mg Sodium

Pictured on page 117.

Kids Can Help

Measuring dry ingredients. Washing fruit. Stirring.

Banana Cake

Creamy orange icing tops this moist cake lightly spiced with cinnamon.

Hard margarine (or butter), softened	1/2 cup	125 mL
Granulated sugar	2/3 cup	150 mL
Large eggs	2	2
Medium bananas, mashed	3	3
Milk	2 tbsp.	30 mL
All-purpose flour	1 1/2 cups	375 mL
Baking powder	1 tbsp.	15 mL
Ground cinnamon	1 tsp.	5 mL
CREAM CHEESE ICING		
Block of cream cheese, softened	4 oz.	125 g
Hard margarine (or butter), softened	2 tbsp.	30 mL
Icing (confectioner's) sugar	1 1/2 cups	375 mL
Grated orange zest	1 tsp.	5 mL

Cream margarine and sugar in large bowl. Add eggs 1 at a time, beating well after each addition.

Add banana and milk. Beat well.

Combine flour, baking powder and cinnamon in medium bowl. Add to banana mixture. Stir until just moistened. Spread evenly in greased 8 inch (20 cm) springform pan. Bake in 350°F (175°C) oven for about 45 minutes until wooden pick inserted in centre of cake comes out clean. Let stand in pan for 5 minutes before removing to wire rack to cool completely.

Cream Cheese Icing: Beat cream cheese and margarine in separate medium bowl until smooth.

Add icing sugar and zest. Beat well. Makes about 1 cup (250 mL) icing. Spread evenly over top of cake. Freezes well. Cuts into 12 wedges.

1 wedge: 334 Calories; 14.8 g Total Fat (7.9 g Mono, 1.3 g Poly, 4.7 g Sat); 47 mg Cholesterol; 48 g Carbohydrate; 1 g Fibre; 4 g Protein; 253 mg Sodium

Pictured on page 117.

Kids Can Help

Measuring dry ingredients. Mashing bananas. Icing the cake.

School Day Brownies

Not too rich or too sweet. Crisp top with a chewy centre—the ultimate brownie.

Brown sugar, packed	3/4 cup	175 mL
Granulated sugar	3/4 cup	175 mL
Hard margarine (or butter)	2/3 cup	150 mL
Large eggs, fork-beaten	3	3
All-purpose flour	3/4 cup	175 mL
Cocoa, sifted if lumpy	1/3 cup	75 mL
Baking powder	1/2 tsp.	2 mL

Icing (confectioner's) sugar, for dusting
   (optional)

Combine first 3 ingredients in large saucepan. Heat and stir on medium until margarine is melted. Remove from heat. Let stand for 10 minutes.

Add eggs. Stir well.

Add flour, cocoa and baking powder. Stir well. Spread evenly in greased 9 x 9 inch (22 x 22 cm) pan. Bake in 350°F (175°C) oven for 30 minutes. Cover with foil. Bake for about 20 minutes until wooden pick inserted in centre comes out moist but not wet with batter. Do not overbake. Discard foil. Let stand in pan on wire rack until almost cooled.

Dust with icing sugar. Freezes well. Cuts into 16 brownies.

1 brownie: 193 Calories; 9.3 g Total Fat (5.7 g Mono, 1 g Poly, 2.1 g Sat); 40 mg Cholesterol; 27 g Carbohydrate; 1 g Fibre; 2 g Protein; 123 mg Sodium

Pictured on page 117.

Kids Can Help

Beating eggs. Measuring dry ingredients. Stirring.
Dusting brownies with icing sugar.

Top: Banana Cake, page 115
Centre: School Day Brownies, above
Bottom: Apple Blueberry Muffins, page 114

Measurement Tables

Throughout this book measurements are given in Conventional and Metric measure. To compensate for differences between the two measurements due to rounding, a full metric measure is not always used. The cup used is the standard 8 fluid ounce. Temperature is given in degrees Fahrenheit and Celsius. Baking pan measurements are in inches and centimetres as well as quarts and litres. An exact metric conversion is given below as well as the working equivalent (Metric Standard Measure).

Spoons

Conventional Measure	Metric Exact Conversion Millilitre (mL)	Metric Standard Measure Millilitre (mL)
1/8 teaspoon (tsp.)	0.6 mL	0.5 mL
1/4 teaspoon (tsp.)	1.2 mL	1 mL
1/2 teaspoon (tsp.)	2.4 mL	2 mL
1 teaspoon (tsp.)	4.7 mL	5 mL
2 teaspoons (tsp.)	9.4 mL	10 mL
1 tablespoon (tbsp.)	14.2 mL	15 mL

Cups

Conventional Measure	Metric Exact Conversion Millilitre (mL)	Metric Standard Measure Millilitre (mL)
1/4 cup (4 tbsp.)	56.8 mL	60 mL
1/3 cup (5 1/3 tbsp.)	75.6 mL	75 mL
1/2 cup (8 tbsp.)	113.7 mL	125 mL
2/3 cup (10 2/3 tbsp.)	151.2 mL	150 mL
3/4 cup (12 tbsp.)	170.5 mL	175 mL
1 cup (16 tbsp.)	227.3 mL	250 mL
4 1/2 cups	1022.9 mL	1000 mL (1 L)

Oven Temperatures

Fahrenheit (°F)	Celsius (°C)
175°	80°
200°	95°
225°	110°
250°	120°
275°	140°
300°	150°
325°	160°
350°	175°
375°	190°
400°	205°
425°	220°
450°	230°
475°	240°
500°	260°

Dry Measurements

Conventional Measure Ounces (oz.)	Metric Exact Conversion Grams (g)	Metric Standard Measure Grams (g)
1 oz.	28.3 g	28 g
2 oz.	56.7 g	57 g
3 oz.	85.0 g	85 g
4 oz.	113.4 g	125 g
5 oz.	141.7 g	140 g
6 oz.	170.1 g	170 g
7 oz.	198.4 g	200 g
8 oz.	226.8 g	250 g
16 oz.	453.6 g	500 g
32 oz.	907.2 g	1000 g (1 kg)

Pans

Conventional Inches	Metric Centimetres
8x8 inch	20x20 cm
9x9 inch	22x22 cm
9x13 inch	22x33 cm
10x15 inch	25x38 cm
11x17 inch	28x43 cm
8x2 inch round	20x5 cm
9x2 inch round	22x5 cm
10x4 1/2 inch tube	25x11 cm
8x4x3 inch loaf	20x10x7.5 cm
9x5x3 inch loaf	22x12.5x7.5 cm

Casseroles

CANADA & BRITAIN Standard Size Casserole	Exact Metric Measure	UNITED STATES Standard Size Casserole	Exact Metric Measure
1 qt. (5 cups)	1.13 L	1 qt. (4 cups)	900 mL
1 1/2 qts. (7 1/2 cups)	1.69 L	1 1/2 qts. (6 cups)	1.35 L
2 qts. (10 cups)	2.25 L	2 qts. (8 cups)	1.8 L
2 1/2 qts. (12 1/2 cups)	2.81 L	2 1/2 qts. (10 cups)	2.25 L
3 qts. (15 cups)	3.38 L	3 qts. (12 cups)	2.7 L
4 qts. (20 cups)	4.5 L	4 qts. (16 cups)	3.6 L
5 qts. (25 cups)	5.63 L	5 qts. (20 cups)	4.5 L

Recipe Index

Company's Coming cookbooks are available at retail locations throughout Canada!

EXCLUSIVE mail order offer on next page

Buy any 2 cookbooks—choose a 3rd FREE of equal or lesser value than the lowest price paid.

Original Series — CA$15.99 Canada — US$12.99 USA & International

CODE		CODE		CODE	
SQ	150 Delicious Squares	MAM	Make-Ahead Meals	RL	Recipes For Leftovers
CA	Casseroles	PB	The Potato Book	EB	The Egg Book
MU	Muffins & More	CCLFC	Low-Fat Cooking	SDPP	School Days Party Pack
SA	Salads	CFK	Cook For Kids	HS	Herbs & Spices
AP	Appetizers	SCH	Stews, Chilies & Chowders	BEV	The Beverage Book
SS	Soups & Sandwiches	FD	Fondues	SCD	Slow Cooker Dinners
CO	Cookies	CCBE	The Beef Book	WM	30-Minute Weekday Meals
PA	Pasta	RC	The Rookie Cook	SDL	School Days Lunches
BA	Barbecues	RHR	Rush-Hour Recipes	PD	Potluck Dishes
PR	Preserves	SW	Sweet Cravings	GBR	Ground Beef Recipes
CH	Chicken, Etc.	YRG	Year-Round Grilling	FRIR	4-Ingredient Recipes
CT	Cooking For Two	GG	Garden Greens	KHC	Kids' Healthy Cooking
SC	Slow Cooker Recipes	CHC	Chinese Cooking	MM	Mostly Muffins
SF	Stir-Fry	PK	The Pork Book		◀NEW▶ September 1/06

3-in-1 Cookbook Collection

CODE	CA$29.99 Canada US$24.99 USA & International
QEE	Quick & Easy Entertaining
MNT	Meals in No Time
	◀NEW▶ August 1/06

Cookbook Author Biography

CODE	CA$15.99 Canada US$12.99 USA & International
JP	Jean Paré: An Appetite for Life

Special Occasion Series

CODE	CA$20.99 Canada US$19.99 USA & International
GFK	Gifts from the Kitchen

CODE	CA$24.99 Canada US$19.99 USA & International
BSS	Baking—Simple to Sensational
CGFK	Christmas Gifts from the Kitchen
TR	Timeless Recipes for All Occasions

CODE	CA$27.99 Canada US$22.99 USA & International
CCEL	Christmas Celebrations
	◀NEW▶ October 1/06

Lifestyle Series

CODE	CA$17.99 Canada US$15.99 USA & International
DC	Diabetic Cooking

CODE	CA$19.99 Canada US$15.99 USA & International
DDI	Diabetic Dinners
LCR	Low-Carb Recipes
HR	Easy Healthy Recipes

Most Loved Recipe Collection

CODE	CA$23.99 Canada US$19.99 USA & International
MLA	Most Loved Appetizers
MLT	Most Loved Treats
MLBQ	Most Loved Barbecuing
MLCO	Most Loved Cookies

CODE	CA$24.99 Canada US$19.99 USA & International
MLSD	Most Loved Salads & Dressings
MLCA	Most Loved Casseroles
	◀NEW▶ November 1/06

Order **ONLINE** for fast delivery!

Log onto **www.companyscoming.com**, browse through our library of cookbooks, gift sets and newest releases and place your order using our fast and secure online order form.

Title	Code	Quantity	Price	Total
			$	$

TOTAL BOOKS (including FREE)		**TOTAL BOOKS PURCHASED:**	$	

	International	Canada & USA
Shipping & Handling First Book (per destination)	$ 11.98 (one book)	$ 5.98 (one book)
Additional Books (include FREE books)	$ ($4.99 each)	$ ($1.99 each)
Sub-Total	$	$
Canadian residents add GST/HST		$
TOTAL AMOUNT ENCLOSED	$	$

Terms

- All orders must be prepaid. Sorry, no CODs.
- Prices are listed in Canadian Funds for Canadian orders, or US funds for US & International orders.
- Prices are subject to change without prior notice.
- Canadian residents must pay GST/HST (no provincial tax required).
- No tax is required for orders outside Canada.
- Satisfaction is guaranteed or return within 30 days for a full refund.
- Make cheque or money order payable to: **Company's Coming Publishing Limited** 2311-96 Street, Edmonton, Alberta Canada T6N 1G3.
- Orders are shipped surface mail. For courier rates, visit our website: **www.companyscoming.com** or contact us: **Tel: 780-450-6223 Fax: 780-450-1857.**

Gift Giving

- Let us help you with your gift giving!
- We will send cookbooks directly to the recipients of your choice if you give us their names and addresses.
- Please specify the titles you wish to send to each person.
- If you would like to include a personal note or card, we will be pleased to enclose it with your gift order.
- Company's Coming Cookbooks make excellent gifts: birthdays, bridal showers, Mother's Day, Father's Day, graduation or any occasion ...collect them all!

☐ **MasterCard**   ☐ **VISA**   Expiry ___/___ MO/YR

Credit Card # _____

Name of cardholder _____

Cardholder signature _____

Shipping Address Send the cookbooks listed above to:

☐ **Please check if this is a Gift Order**

Name: _____

Street: _____

City: _____ Prov./State: _____

Postal Code/Zip: _____ Country: _____

Tel: (___) _____

E-mail address: _____

Your privacy is important to us. We will not share your e-mail address or personal information with any outside party.

☐ **YES! Please add me to your News Bite e-mail newsletter.**

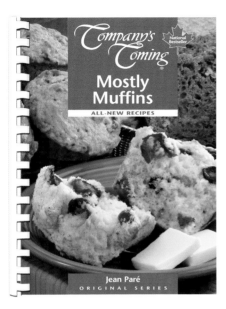

Revel in the welcoming aroma of fresh baking! *Mostly Muffins* offers more than 120 all-new recipes, perfect for fast breakfasts, delicious coffee breaks and tasty supper sides. Whip up these easy quick breads—from muffins and loaves to biscuits and scones—tonight!

Company's Coming COOKBOOKS®

Quick & Easy Recipes

Everyday Ingredients

Canada's **most popular cookbooks!**